Effectiveness of Screened, Demand-Driven **Job Training Programs** for Disadvantaged Workers

An Evaluation of the New Orleans Career Pathway Training

Matthew D. Baird, John Engberg, Gabriella C. Gonzalez, Thomas Goughnour, Italo A. Gutierrez, Rita Karam

T0289448

EDUCATION AND LABOR

Sponsored by the U.S. Department of Labor

For more information on this publication, visit www.rand.org/t/RR2980

Library of Congress Cataloging-in-Publication Data is available for this publication.
ISBN: 978-1-9774-0347-6

Published (2019) by the RAND Corporation, Santa Monica, Calif.

RAND® is a registered trademark.

*Cover: anandaBGD/Getty Images (top left). Dean Mitchell/Getty Images (top right).
recep-bg/Getty Images (bottom).*

Support RAND
Make a tax-deductible charitable contribution at
www.rand.org/giving/contribute

www.rand.org

Preface

In efforts to improve how the U.S. workforce is trained and employed, the U.S. Department of Labor (DOL) has set aside grant money for local governments to implement innovative programs, through the Workforce Innovation Fund (WIF). As part of these grants, local governments are required to solicit and hire external, independent evaluators of those programs. In 2014, the city of New Orleans bid on the second round of WIF grants for a Type B "Promising Ideas" project for programs with some prior evidence of effectiveness that require further and more-rigorous evidence before scaling up significantly. The city was awarded approximately $5.8 million for a five-year implementation of a prescreened, demand-driven job training program, which included resources for implementation and external evaluation. The RAND Corporation bid on the opportunity to be the third-party evaluator and was awarded the evaluation subcontract at the end of 2014.

This report was funded with federal funds under a grant awarded by the DOL's Employment and Training Administration. The content of this publication does not necessarily reflect the views of the policies of the U.S. Department of Labor, nor does mention of trade names, commercial products, or organizations imply any endorsement of same by the U.S. government.

This report, which details the final findings in evaluating the program, includes three primary elements: an implementation analysis, an outcome analysis, and a cost-benefit analysis. While this report is written primarily for the benefit of the DOL, it should additionally be of special interest to local workforce investment boards and state governments, as well as philanthropic foundations interested in investments in human capital targeting low-income workers.

This report has an online-only appendix that contains the survey instruments and other relevant information. This can be found at www.rand.org/t/rr2980.

This study was undertaken by RAND Education and Labor, a division of the RAND Corporation that conducts research on early childhood through postsecondary education programs, workforce development, and programs and policies affecting workers, entrepreneurship, and financial literacy and decisionmaking.

More information about RAND can be found at www.rand.org. Questions about this report should be directed to mbaird@rand.org, and questions about RAND Education and Labor should be directed to educationandlabor@rand.org.

Contents

Figures

Tables

Summary

The economic landscape in the United States has changed over the past 30 years, and the demand for workers with higher-level technical skills continues to grow. Unfortunately, employers in many regions of the country find that the skills of the available workforce in their areas do not match their needs. Because of this, important positions are left unfilled for long periods of time. Moreover, unskilled workers face a shrinking pool of employment opportunities. Wage and opportunity gaps are widening between those who have in-demand skills and those who do not.

Understanding how these challenges play out, the city of New Orleans' Office of Workforce Development (OWD) developed a job training program with a grant from the U.S. Department of Labor (DOL) Workforce Innovation Fund (WIF) awarded in 2014. The program, Career Pathways, was designed to help lower-skilled unemployed, underemployed, and discouraged individuals train for and find skilled jobs in advanced manufacturing (AM) and energy, medical care, and information technology (IT).

Researchers from the RAND Corporation were asked to assess the ways in which the program was implemented and evaluate its effectiveness for workers and hiring firms as well as its overall costs and benefits. For better identification of the effects of the program, the training was implemented as a randomized controlled trial. The research team collected and analyzed information from many sources at each stage of the study and found meaningful positive results in a number of areas, including wage growth, suggestive evidence of increased job satisfaction, and a large return on investment in terms of cost versus benefit of the program. The effects on other outcomes, such as employment and duration, were not statistically significant. These findings elicited a number of recommendations and lessons learned that will be of interest not only to OWD, but to other workforce investment boards (WIBs), policymakers, organizations, and employers concerned with workforce development.

About Career Pathways

Career Pathways sought to offer job-specific technical training in electrical, welding, and pipefitting professions (advanced manufacturing industry); medical coding and billing professions; pharmacy technicians (health care industry); and in IT more generally. There were three distinct stages of the Career Pathways program:

1. **Recruitment and screening.** Several recruitment tools were used, including online campaigns and fixed tablet stations at targeted local city hotspots. Interested candidates then participated in a screening process that included some combination of a program orientation, drug testing, completion of a relevant assignment and/or test, and an interview. Screeners evaluated candidates' interest in the career options offered, as well as their likelihood for successfully completing the training program.

2. **Training.** Training providers worked with local firms in the target industries to develop appropriate curricula. There were 25 cohorts, consisting of 367 trainees, who were offered up to two rounds of training. The first round of training lasted approximately two months, with courses taking place four hours a day, five days a week on average. After successful completion, most trainees were given the option to enter a subsequent "stackable" credit program, an additional two months of training within their career pathway. After entering the training program, each candidate was allotted $6,000 of credit that could be used for books, equipment, transportation costs, and other training-related needs.

3. **Coordination with hiring firms.** Trainees were not guaranteed employment upon completion of the program. Instead, the goal was to direct new trainees to potential employers in the area, where they could apply for positions related to their recent training.

Findings: Program Implementation

Our team designed a process evaluation to examine how various partners implemented the Career Pathways program, the extent to which the program was implemented as initially proposed, and the structural and logistical challenges that stakeholders faced. We collected information from stakeholders through interviews and focus groups. Stakeholders included OWD, other city government agencies, training providers, employers, and trainees.

Partnerships between OWD, training providers, and employers were key. OWD, training providers, and employers commented that the partnerships between stakeholders were strong and valuable. Employers, in particular, reported strong working relationships with OWD and training providers and that they felt that their employment needs were taken into consideration.

There were difficulties in having small local partners or firms in feeder industries conduct prescreening for job training. The original program design intended for firms in the hospitality and leisure industry, as well as cultural partners in the community, to screen potential trainees from their pool of employees and members. Neither relationship ended up working, because the firms were unwilling to determine and then supply their more-reliable employees for training in other fields, and the community partners were intent on approving any member with interest and still not providing enough candidates. Ultimately, screening was brought in-house to OWD, which worked much better.

Employers valued trainees' program experience. Employers also offered anecdotal evidence about the higher-level quality of trainees compared with other employees in similar jobs in their business. They noted WIF trainees had stronger content knowledge when starting and seemed to know what to expect while on the job.

Trainees expressed a desire for more hands-on experience. Across the cohorts and sectors, trainees reported that the program did not provide them with as much real work experience as they would have preferred. They viewed the pathway as having helped them obtain accreditation for entry-level positions but lacking adequate opportunities to apply what they learned in real settings. Electrical and pipefitters' trainees especially noted that having more time doing hands-on practice while in the course would have been beneficial.

Trainees and training providers were aware that training was only for entry-level positions. Focus-group members also expressed a desire for the course to be extended so they could learn more and be more competitive when seeking work in the field. Training providers noted that the courses were meant only to whet the appetite of trainees—if they wanted more education, they could remain in a program. They also understood that the entry-level course might be inadequate for the job market.

Trainees and employers wanted more flexibility and "soft skills" in training. In focus-group discussions, trainees spoke about the lack of flexibility in the curriculum and instruction, noting that there was little individualized instruction. It should be noted that IT trainees participated in online-only training. Employers, on the other hand, indicated that "soft skills"—such as showing up every day on time, following instructions, and problem-solving—need to be stressed in training. Employers also noted a need for a task comfort-level question during the screening and application process to make sure that applicants were aware of and comfortable with the physical expectations of work.

Communication of program benefits to trainees could be improved. Many trainees noted that they were unaware of stipends, materials, and other benefits until late in their programs. Some also noted that support was inadequate. In some cohorts, participants were not allowed to work while they were enrolled in the training although many did work and earn money, according to employment records.

Job counseling and employer engagement could be improved.
More than half of surveyed training participants reported receiving
job opportunity information from OWD compared with a third of
nonparticipants surveyed. Similarly, about 40 percent received resume-
development and job-readiness services, compared with 30 percent and
23 percent of nonparticipants, respectively. OWD services, however,
did not fully facilitate participant-employer connections.

Findings: Program Outcomes

The research team used a randomized controlled trial to assess program
outcomes. There were over 500 individuals who consented to participate in the study. The program was set up so that a person assigned to
be in the control group for a given cohort could enter into a later randomization cohort to try to receive training.

    Participation and completion rates were relatively high. The
attendance rate for the first round of training was high; 83 percent of
individuals assigned to a training group attended at least one class session. The attendance rate for the optional second round of training was
substantially lower at 20 percent, though this number includes cohorts
that did not have a second round of training. Of the 83 percent that
attended at least one session, 77.8 percent completed training, for an
overall completion rate of 64.4 percent.

    **Individuals in the training group who completed the pro-
gram, on average, went on to earn higher wages.** The first two
cohorts were not successful in producing higher earnings; indeed,
the estimated impact for them was negative, though not statistically
significant. However, the remaining 13 cohorts for which there were
post-training earnings data showed meaningful earnings increases of
approximately $804 per quarter of a year, which was statistically sig-
nificant. Those who did not participate in the program (the control
group) earned approximately $3,317 per quarter in the post-training
period. A comparison between the two groups suggests that those who
were assigned to receive training received an approximately 25-percent
increase in earnings.

Health care trainees had the greatest increase in wages. When compared with trainees focusing in other sectors, those in health care had the most considerable returns in terms of quarterly earnings. The two cohorts for which the team had data for earned just over $1,900 more than trainees in other groups per quarter. However, this finding should be reviewed with caution. The addition of later quarters of post-training earnings from these and later cohorts could result in important revisions to this average estimate.

There were no effects of the program on the likelihood to be employed or job duration. We found no difference between those invited to be trained and those in the control group with respect to later employment or job duration.

IT trainees were more likely to find jobs in their fields. There was an overall significant increase in the proportion of IT trainees who found a job working in IT after they completed the program. There was a large increase in the proportion of health care trainees finding work in health care as well, though this effect was not statistically significant. There were no substantial effects from the training in terms of increasing employment for those in the advanced manufacturing industries.

Training group workers' overall job satisfaction improved. After the end of training, trainees and control persons were asked the degree to which they were satisfied with their job. Most trainees agreed or strongly agreed that they were satisfied, and had higher job satisfaction than those randomly assigned to the control group, though this was based on a small sample size of responders. The increased job satisfaction for those assigned training was highest for those who reported that training helped them in their current job or to find a better paying job. However, these results were based on low response rates to the survey: 26 percent for the treatment group and 9 percent for the control group.

There was insufficient evidence of program effects on arrests. We did not find any statistically significant change in arrests between the training and nontraining groups. There was a large decrease in arrests for men, but this result was not statistically significant.

Peers had a positive effect on each other. There was evidence that trainee peers ultimately influenced one another in positive ways. Specifically, individuals whose fellow trainees had a better history of employment were more likely to be placed into jobs at the end of the program. They were also more likely to have better earnings. This may be due to a better classroom environment, networking creating better opportunities after training, or both.

Those who entered training with the lowest earnings and who were unemployed had the largest earnings increases over their counterparts in the control group. Those that were unemployed before training had an earnings increase of $2,367 a quarter over the unemployed non-trainees, while those with annual incomes below $5,000 before training had an increase of $1,304.

Screening interviews were not necessarily effective. Initial screening sought to pinpoint individuals who would be more likely to stay in the training program. However, when the research team compared the outcomes for those who rated lower and higher in the interview scores, they found little difference in either program attrition or outcomes. On the other hand, the basic literacy and numeracy test given during the screening did demonstrate some accuracy for predicting program success as well as higher gains for earnings.

The program had a favorable return on investment—eventually. Table S.1 summarizes the benefits and costs associated with the WIF program from the perspective of the participants, the public, and society.

As Table S.1 shows, the benefits of the program immediately exceed the costs for participants in the later cohorts, given their increased earnings. For the public sector, it takes five years to make up the implementation costs in terms of decreased welfare transfers and increased tax returns. For society, it takes three years for benefits to exceed costs, including bearing the societal cost of the first two cohorts with earning losses. This makes this overall intervention favorable with respect to ROI, especially as this is a conservative estimate—it does not account for all of the realized benefits, such as improved job satisfaction and potential decreases in arrests for men.

Table S.1
Benefits, Costs, and Rate of Return for the Average Participant

		Participant (2016 cohorts)	Participant (2017 and later cohorts)	Public	Society
3-year horizon	Net Benefits/Costs	−$16,781	$7,285	−$2,879	$2,001
	IRR (quarterly real rate)	N/A	N/A	−6.46%	10.74%
	ROI (annualized rate)	−360.01%	355.28%	−14.88%	7.99%
30-year horizon	Net Benefits/Costs	−$16,781	$44,564	$16,476	$58,634
	IRR (quarterly real rate)	N/A	N/A	5.72%	15.93%
	ROI (annualized rate)	−210.03%	23.57%	3.95%	7.44%
Break-even year		Never	Year 1	Year 5	Year 3

NOTE: Dollar figures are adjusted for inflation to 2018. The internal rate of return (IRR) is the discount rate that makes the net present value of all cash flows equal to zero while the return on investment (ROI) measures the amount of return on a particular investment, relative to the investment's cost. Chapter 5 and Appendix C of the report provide a detailed explanation of the methodology used to estimate the costs and benefits of the program

Recommendations

Career Pathways was ultimately successful in a number of areas, but as with any workforce development program, there were areas that could be improved. While our findings may not be necessarily generalizable to other urban locations that do not share the same employment conditions and other contextual characteristics of New Orleans, the following recommendations can still be considered by program leaders and employer and organization stakeholders, as well as similar groups throughout the country seeking to develop such programs.

Consider more intentionally deploying two- to four- month job training programs for unemployed and low-income individuals. Increased earnings were most prominent among these populations.

Incorporate hands-on practice and classroom instruction when feasible. The provision of fully online training to the program population enrolled in the IT pathway is potentially concerning. Online programs, such as the one that IT trainees engaged in, have many benefits. However, this mode of instruction might not have been the most effective for a vulnerable population that might have multiple competing demands and limited professional experience. Blended approaches to instruction might be a better option because they have the potential to address the issues of nontraditional students with unique needs during the part of instruction that occurs in class.

Create strong and sustainable partnerships between government and nongovernment entities. The ability to build such partnerships is affected by funding constraints and changes in the economic and political contexts in which the partnerships are embedded. However, OWD responded effectively to lessons learned along the way.

Ensure that training programs are connected to local demand and that there are strong industry partnerships. The demand-driven aspect of the training program was likely critical to its success; the connections with local firms allowed OWD the agility to switch pathways after the energy sector demand dried up. However, more could have been done in the training to connect workers with local firms. Local WIBs can form meaningful industry partnerships and buy-in that allows for post-training introductions and support.

Be able to respond to an evolving job market. The program was initially designed to develop workers for the energy sector as well as advanced manufacturing. However, decreasing oil prices in 2015 and 2016 led to reduction in demand for energy workers, and program leaders chose to focus instead on the IT and health care sectors, in addition to advanced manufacturing. Any job-training program therefore should be flexible enough to respond to local demand shifts in a timely manner.

Communicate nonwage as well as wage and employment benefits of a program. Most evaluations of job training programs are limited to employment status and earning outcomes. Calculating only these outcomes would have missed the gains in job satisfaction. Further work is necessary to understand the impact on arrests.

Take time to get it right. Analysis suggested that the outcomes from Career Pathways improved after the first few trainee cohorts. If the program had been evaluated simply on the initial cohorts, it would have been viewed as an ineffective intervention. The city and training providers needed to learn, through trial and error, the best approaches for recruitment, industry partnerships, and screening decisions.

Have patience when seeking investment returns. The positive returns to society suggest that this program demonstrates a good use of public resources and could potentially be a model for future training programs. However, some patience is required. The first two cohorts had earnings losses, and the program did not have benefits exceed costs for the government until five years after the start of the program, though for society overall it only took three years.

Acknowledgments

We are grateful for the assistance we have received on this project. We would like to note the help we received from the New Orleans Office of Workforce Development and the New Orleans Workforce Development Board, including Brandi Ebanks, Tammie Washington, Sunae Villavaso, and Sabrina Johnson; we also appreciate the feedback and help we received from Abt Associates and the National Evaluation Coordinator, including Rachel Cook and Eliza Kean. We are thankful for the considerable amount of work done by Elizabeth Thornton on this project. Kathryn Edwards and Fatih Unlu of the RAND Corporation and Stephen Bell of Westat provided reviews that ensured our work met RAND's high standards for quality, and we express our gratitude for their careful work and helpful feedback. We are grateful for Benjamin Horwitz's assistance with New Orleans Police Department records, and for the help from the Louisiana Workforce Commission, including Danelle Gilkes and Laurence Aiken, in acquiring the employment records. We would like to thank Scroggins LLC and Topp Knotch, both of which provided assistance with focus groups. We appreciate the willingness to sit in on interviews by representatives of the training providers and ResCare. Finally, we are indebted to several other RAND colleagues who helped during this project, notably LaToya Williams and Gary Cecchine, but also William Waggy, Claudia Rodriguez, Goke Akinniranye, Lindsey Polley, Nima Shahidinia, and Etienne Rosas.

Abbreviations

2SLS	two-stage least squares
AGI	adjusted gross income
AM	advanced manufacturing
BLS	Bureau of Labor Statistics
DOL	U.S. Department of Labor
FITAP	Family Independence Temporary Assistance Program
HR	human resources
IT	information technology
IRR	internal rate of return
ITT	intent to treat
KCSP	Kinship Care Subsidy Program
LWC	Louisiana Workforce Commission
NCCER	National Center for Construction Education and Research
NOPD	New Orleans Police Department
obs.	observations
OLS	ordinary least squares
OSHA	Occupational Health and Safety Administration
OWD	Office of Workforce Development (Louisiana)

RCM	resource cost model
RCT	randomized controlled trial
ROI	return on investment
SNAP	Supplemental Nutrition Assistance Program
TABE	Test of Adult Basic Education
TANF	Temporary Assistance for Needy Families
TOT	treatment on the treated
UI	unemployment insurance
WBR	weekly benefit rate
WDB	Workforce Development Board
WIA	Workforce Innovation Act
WIOA	Workforce Innovation and Opportunity Act
WIB	Workforce Investment Board
WIF	Workforce Innovation Fund

## CHAPTER ONE

Introduction

Shifts in the global marketplace have led to the growth of knowledge-based industries, which require workers with higher levels of technical skills. This widening of the gap between skills required and those offered by the present labor force means that companies cannot fill vacancies and grow at their ideal rate, while the wage disparity between high- and low-skilled workers is growing (Acemoglu, 2002). At the same time, workers with few or obsolete skills face diminishing demand and a deteriorating pool of job opportunities. These forces have combined to increase wage and earnings inequality (Autor and Dorn, 2013; Autor, Katz, and Kearney, 2006; Goos, Manning, and Salomons, 2014).

While these trends have advanced, the city of New Orleans' Office of Workforce Development (OWD) received a grant from the U.S. Department of Labor (DOL) Workforce Innovation Fund (WIF) to implement and fund the implementation and evaluation of a job training program for disadvantaged workers to develop human capital in skilled occupations. The project was proposed and funded as a Type B "Promising Ideas" project for programs with some prior evidence of effectiveness that requires further and more rigorous evidence before scaling up significantly. Originally called the "Summer Career Pathways" program, the name was simplified to the "Career Pathways" program when the training scope was expanded from one cohort starting each summer to several cohorts throughout the year. While the nature of the intervention has changed over time, as we discuss in Chapter Three, the main characteristics of the current program are:

(1) multifaceted recruitment of job training candidates to capture as many interested individuals as possible; (2) a rigorous screening mechanism, including a 45-minute scored interview to determine eligibility for training based on perceived likelihood to succeed in the training; (3) integration of adult basic education with occupational skills training; (4) implementation of comprehensive career pathways made up of sequential training and employment opportunities in high-demand skilled areas; and (5) development of partnerships between government and nongovernment entities to improve outcomes for workers and employers, including demand-driven curriculum (training areas and curriculum choices that are determined based on information about local labor demand from industry partners).

The training providers, including community college staff and private-sector training organization staff, met with the intervention's regional hiring firm partners in the career pathways industries (advanced manufacturing [AM]), information technology [IT], and health care) to develop the curriculum to match skills training with the needs of employers. The job training program was designed as a cross-sector pipeline from unemployed or underemployed situations in low-paying sectors of the labor market into higher-paying jobs in these target industries. Screening candidates at the time of their application to take part in the training was expected to enable the selection of the individuals most likely to complete the training program and experience subsequent labor-market success. The curriculum was demand-driven, in the sense that local employers described to OWD and the training providers which skills they needed workers to possess for open positions. The demand-driven curriculum and connections with employers aimed to improve the probability that there would be appropriate jobs at the end of the pipeline.

The RAND Corporation was selected as the independent evaluator of the program and began work in March 2015.

1.1. Research Context and Motivation

The literature on evaluations of job training programs has mixed evidence on program effectiveness, with some programs shown as effective in improving employment and earnings but most not showing positive returns (Van Horn, Edwards, and Greene, 2015). There are three groups of prior research most applicable to this report: evaluations of Workforce Investment Act (WIA)–funded programs (WIA being the predecessor of the Workforce Innovation and Opportunity Act [WIOA], the authorizing act for the WIF program), investigations of demand-driven job training programs, and studies of job training programs with prescreening requirements. We discuss each of these.

The first set of papers that we examine investigate the success of job training programs funded through WIA, to determine whether this funding model and the type of job training programs it funds improve labor outcomes for trainees. A review of these programs provides a benchmark for the present program. Heinrich et al. (2013) evaluate WIA training programs using quasiexperimental design methods in 12 states for up to four years after the start of the programs. They find moderately sized, positive, and statistically significant treatment effects on employment and earnings. For example, they estimate quarterly earnings increases of $591 for women and $419 for men (around a 25 percent and 15 percent increase over base earnings for women and men, respectively). Employment rates see an average increase of around 6 percentage points. Andersson et al. (2013) investigate a different set of WIA programs and find smaller effects. Employment effects are increases of around $300 in quarterly earnings, while the increase in employment rates is around 2 percentage points.

We next discuss the literature dedicated to understanding whether demand-driven industry selection and curriculum development lead to successful job training programs. These demand-driven programs—training programs that are highly integrated with the local labor market and private sector—have been shown to be successful. For example, the Center for Employment and Training in San Jose, California, provided three to six months of vocational training to disadvantaged youths and adults and saw gains in sustained earnings of about

40 percent per year (Heckman, 1999). One of the salient features of the Center for Employment and Training was that it emphasized job skills training over learning basic skills. The program also had strong ties with the local labor market. An industrial advisory board was set up to aid in the skills selection (Heckman, 1999). In this same vein, sectoral employment strategies have taken root in the last 20 years. These strategies consist of implementing services and activities—including job training—that focus on the needs of specific sectors. Specifically, these training programs are based on market-driven strategies of identifying sectors that have unmet needs for workers and then providing training to low-income workers to help them acquire the skills needed to fill the available positions (Rodner, Clymer, and Wyckoff, 2008).

The results obtained in demand-driven training programs are encouraging. For example, Public/Private Ventures, a nonprofit research organization, reported in its Sectoral Employment Impact Study the employment and earning impacts in three training sites (Maguire et al., 2010). These sites were the Jewish Vocational Service in Boston, Massachusetts, which provided training over a period of 21 to 25 weeks, for 20 to 25 hours per week, with a sectoral focus on medical and basic office skills and computerized accounting; Per Scholas, in Bronx, New York, which provided a 15-week, 500-hour computer technician program with a sectoral focus on the IT industry; and the Wisconsin Regional Training Partnership in Milwaukee, Wisconsin, which provided one to four weeks of training for anywhere from 40 to 160 hours, with an initial sectoral focus on health care and construction and manufacturing, and which later extended its offerings to road construction, lead abatement, and commercial driver license preparation. Public/Private Ventures reported that participants in these sector-focused training programs earned 18.3 percent more than those in the control group in the 24-month study period, and 29.3 percent more during months 13 through 24. The gains were derived not only from working more hours but also from higher wages (in the second year, program participants' wages averaged $12.50 per hour, versus $11.75 per hour for controls).

Other positive experiences can be found in Detroit, Michigan, where Focus:HOPE provides machinist-related training targeted to the metalworking industry (Thompson, Turner-Meikeljohn, and Conway, 2000); in the San Francisco and Oakland, California area, where Asian Neighborhood Design provides training targeted to the construction sector, mainly in carpentry and cabinetry (Conway and Bear, 2000); in the Bronx, where Cooperative Home Care Associates trains women in home health care (Inserra, Conway, and Rodat, 2002); and in Chicago, Illinois, where the Jane Addams Resource Corporation provides training courses on specific metalworking occupations, primarily punch-press operator and die-setting–related occupations (Glasmeier, Nelson, and Thompson, 2000). Evidence in favor of sectoral employment strategies also comes from the Sectoral Employment Demonstration, funded by the Employment and Training Administration of DOL, which helps DOL determine whether sector-based strategies could be adopted and used by local workforce investment boards (WIBs). Twelve organizations were awarded 15-month implementation grants to perform specific sectoral interventions. Of these, all but one enrolled participants in training, eight reported successful job placements, and two reported average wage gains of 18 percent or more (Pindus et al., 2004). This literature shows that demand-driven job training programs have a good track record of generating positive labor outcomes for the people they train. We add to this by providing additional evidence toward the hypothesis that demand-driven training programs can generate positive worker outcomes.

Finally, we review the literature on how individuals are selected for public programs (such as job training) and whether the selection mechanisms lead to *screening* (selecting individuals likely to benefit more from the program) or *creaming* (selecting individuals likely to have good outcomes whether or not they are trained). Bell and Orr (2002) reviewed and added to the literature on screening and creaming. They evaluated seven state welfare-to-work programs and found that creaming activities dominate the selection process, with no apparent relationship to the program effectiveness measures that would be increased by useful screening activities. These findings were echoed in a study of the Job Training Partnership Act (Heckman, Heinrich, and Smith, 2011).

There are few examples of evaluations of programs that explicitly use persistence at prior work or training as a screening mechanism for subsequent training. In an earlier RAND Corporation study, De Tray (1980) demonstrates that military service, in addition to providing skill augmentation, serves as an effective screening device that is used by future employers. Eberts, O'Leary, and Wandner (2002) and Berger, Black, and Smith (2001) also investigate how profiling tools can affect the impact of interventions more generally, such as targeting benefits of unemployment insurance programs. Our hypothesis was that OWD's WIF intervention would lead to greater expected benefit by screening for prior demonstration of persistence. We contribute to the literature on programs with screening requirements by further evaluating the extent to which screening of training participants that is based on prior perseverance leads to improved outcomes.

Much of the literature described above uses quasiexperimental design methods. In this report, we are able to leverage a randomized controlled trial (RCT). The empirical case for the use of RCTs and for the fragility of nonexperimental methods to evaluate social programs is made clear in LaLonde (1986). LaLonde uses an experimental evaluation of the National Supported Work Demonstration program as a benchmark against which to compare nonexperimental estimates. He uses several common nonexperimental estimators and obtains a variety of impact estimates, most of which differ substantially from the corresponding experimental estimates. Heckman and Smith (1995) argue that the difference between the experimental and nonexperimental estimates could be reduced significantly by collecting rich data in nonexperimental settings. They also highlight the substantial progress in nonexperimental evaluation methods in the prior two decades.

A more recent summary of experimental evaluation in the context of labor economics is provided by List and Rasul (2011). In their report, they defined a *framed field experiment* (as opposed to, for example, a laboratory experiment) as one that "incorporates important elements of the context of the naturally occurring environment with respect to the commodity, task, stakes, and information set of the subjects" (p. 122). They highlighted the value of evaluations of "packaged" interventions that reflect combinations of actual policies that might be implemented.

They highlighted Kremer, Miguel, and Thornton (2009) and Duflo et al. (2005) as examples of this approach. In our case, the proposed intervention packaged the creation of a career pipeline from the screening through potential training to the hiring firms, as well as training curricula that are driven by unmet sectoral demands. As Levitt and List (2007a, 2007b) acknowledged, there continue to be threats to validity in spite of improved methods and experimental protocols; this is due to the participants' awareness of their role as experimental subjects. RCTs do have their limitations: Primarily, they are at times "black boxes," showing whether an intervention was successful without necessarily shedding light on why or how it succeeded, limiting replication (see List and Rasul, 2011, Heckman and Smith, 1995, and Heckman, 1999, for a discussion of these limitations). However, experimental estimates continue to be the gold standard in estimating causal effects.

Our work offers several other contributions to the lines of research summarized above. First, we use an experimental evaluation that has clear and strong identification of the effect of the program, which has rarely been applied to demand-driven training programs.

Second, one typical feature of experimental evaluations is that they only allow the evaluator to estimate whether a program works. This is a valuable feature when the package of interventions mimics actual policy proposals. However, this alone cannot provide an explanation of why the program works or why it does not. In other words, experimental designs can be characterized as a "black box" for empirically determining the impact of a program (Heckman and Smith, 1995). To go beyond this and be able to look into the black box, we also used in-depth interviews and focus groups with key stakeholders of the program: trainees, screening organizations, employers in the advanced manufacturing (AM) and energy sectors, and trainers and instructors at the selected training provider. These interviews and focus groups provided valuable insights on what the main challenges were during the implementation of the program, whether the program was useful to participants, whether employers were satisfied with the program, and which aspects could be changed to improve either the training for the next cohort or the design of future workforce development programs. Though this type of analysis does not provide evidence that allows for causal inference about mechanisms, when conducted in the context of a program that is shown to have a positive impact on outcomes, this analysis helps generate hypotheses that can be tested in later interventions.

Third, we are able to examine the effectiveness of a screening mechanism built specifically for this training program (not done to our knowledge in any experimental evaluation of a job training program). We evaluate the effect of the screening mechanism on program participation (e.g., attendance, completion, and credentialing) as well as on post-training outcomes, such as employment and earnings.

Finally, this report adds to the literature by looking at important secondary outcomes, such as arrests and job satisfaction, which has not widely been done in the literature examining RCTs of job training programs. This provides a more complete view into the effectiveness of the program.

1.2. Overview of Program

In this section, we discuss the program as it was eventually implemented. This differs in some important ways from the initially proposed program, as we discuss at length in Chapter 3. The final version of the intervention provided job-specific training in electrical, welding, and pipefitting pathways in the AM industry; IT; and medical coding and billing and pharmacy technician pathways in the health care industry. The intervention had three distinct stages: (1) recruitment and screening, (2) a two-month core demand-driven training program that was followed by the possibility of an additional two-month "stackable" credit program, and (3) the goal (sometimes unmet) of coordination with industry firms after training.

Screened recruitment. The first objective of the program was to access a population of jobseekers (unemployed, underemployed, discouraged, and other interested workers), who had potential to succeed in both training and subsequent work situations. A prescreened population—one that has been well informed about the available career pathways, rigor of the training program, and employment possibilities postcompletion, and which has demonstrated evidence for higher rates of completion of the training through their preparedness for training—could have a higher likelihood of persistence in the program.

To maximize outreach in recruitment, OWD worked with an outreach company and assigned a staff member to exclusively oversee recruitment activities. The city of New Orleans has established a system of "opportunity centers," which administered candidate screening. These five centers are traditional workforce development agencies that have the capacity to assess workforce readiness skills and provide workforce readiness case management to candidates.

Participants were recruited in several ways: (1) one-stop centers that provided program information to individuals receiving government assistance programs (e.g., Supplemental Nutrition Assistance Program, unemployment insurance), including individuals required to partake in career readiness and reporting activities under the federal funding mandate; (2) fixed tablet stations at targeted local hotspots throughout the city (e.g., community centers, public assistance offices) that provided program information and collected information on interested applicants; (3) general program outreach and outreach targeting particular populations (e.g., low-skill hospitality workers) via paid advertising and online marketing campaigns; and (4) recruitment from OWD's community partners who cohosted a series of workshops, which were open to both referrals and members of the general public, to provide interested candidates with program information.

After recruitment, interested candidates participated in a screening process that ultimately included four components: (1) attendance at a mandatory orientation; (2) drug testing (and, in some cases, a criminal background check, depending on whether the industry partners in the given pathway required it); (3) completion of a relevant assignment and/or test, such as the Test of Adult Basic Education (TABE) or the Wonderlic test; and (4) completion of a structured interview. Based on these components, OWD gauged candidates' interest in the career pathways and their likelihood of successfully completing the training program, assigned them a score from a scoring rubric of their interview, and accepted those scoring above a certain threshold.

The screening was intended not to eliminate candidates from any government training or assistance (unless they self-selected to opt themselves out), but rather served as a method of assessment of the cohort's collective literacy and numeracy skills, which would be used to inform and customize the training curriculum and individuals' fitness for training, depending on such things as historic job dependability, transportation to training, and childcare in place. Candidates who were deemed as "not ready" for training based on the results of these tests were referred to other OWD-administered assistance and training programs.

Once candidates completed the components of this screening process, potential trainees were invited to attend a seminar during which they received detailed information about the program and participating in the evaluation. Candidates who were interested in proceeding were required to complete a program participation consent form and baseline survey in order to be eligible for training (via the randomization). After collecting all consent forms and baseline surveys, we randomly assigned those who received an offer to participation in the training program, as described below.

Training. The Career Pathways training program represented a coordinated effort of OWD, the training providers, and firms in the relevant sectors to develop a demand-driven curriculum designed to teach technical skills that employers were seeking in their workers. The training providers worked with local firms in the target industries (AM, IT, and health care) to develop the curriculum where necessary. OWD also engaged potential employers through trade advisory committees, which met quarterly, to obtain an understanding of workforce requirements and hiring potential

The first round of training for each cohort lasted approximately two months (depending on the career pathway, such as electrical, IT, or medical coding and billing; see Table 2.2 in Chapter 2 for details on each cohort and its pathway) with courses taking place an average of four hours a day, five days a week. The exact number of classes associated with each pathway varied each year depending on the preferences of trainees, as program participants self-selected into their desired pathway. The short duration of the training served both as a challenge (skills desired may take significantly longer to develop) and an opportunity (workers will be more likely to be able to afford the opportunity costs of not working during a shorter training).

Upon entry into the training program, each candidate was allotted $6,000 worth of training credits, which could be used for books, equipment, transportation costs, and other associated costs related to the program. At the completion of the first core training, most of the training cohorts were given the option to enter a subsequent "stackable" credit program, which was an additional two months of training within the career pathway. This training program did not fund any further training past this second round; however, trainees who were interested in advancing their credentials could opt to receive funding through other programs or by paying out-of-pocket tuition costs.

If trainees did not complete or attend the training, they were still included in the evaluation because training completion is one of our outcomes of interest. All individuals who entered the randomization process are included in the intent-to-treat (ITT) analysis of the impact of getting the offer to participate in training.

Coordination with hiring firms. The end of the pipeline sought to direct the new trainees to potential employers in the area, and the ultimate goal was for the firms in the relevant industries to be more likely to employ trainees from this program due to its screening component and firmly coordinated training curriculum. Trainees, however, were not guaranteed employment after completing the program; completion of the training constituted completion of treatment, while employment is an outcome of the evaluation.

Potential hiring firms were, at times, engaged to provide information on their workforce needs and participate in the curriculum development process, and there was a possibility for the training itself to include an on-the-job training component if requested by a hiring firm partner, though this occurred rarely. This component was intended to not exceed a period of seven weeks, in order to allow for the evaluation to take place with sufficient follow-up time.

The goal was that this training program would provide dependable, skilled workers to firms in the relevant industries, provide cost-effective targeted training to a prescreened population, and raise the earnings of discouraged, unemployed, and underemployed workers.

1.3. Target Populations

For most of our analyses, the individual is the unit of analysis. The main population of interest consists of individuals who are not satisfied with their current employment situation and have the potential to succeed in both training and subsequent employment in the advance manufacturing, health care, and IT sectors. These include unemployed, underemployed, and discouraged workers. Among those interested, eligibility was determined by passing a test of basic literacy and numeracy, as well as a screening interview that was scored to determine suitability for training.

Unemployed persons (current population survey): The group was made up of persons ages 16 years and older who had no employment during the reference week, were available for work (except for in the case of temporary illness), and had made specific efforts to find employment sometime during the four-week period ending with the reference week. Those who were waiting to be recalled to a job from which they had been laid off need not have been looking for work to be classified as unemployed.

Underemployed workers: The Bureau of Labor Statistics (BLS) in the DOL defines underemployed individuals as involuntary part-time workers (BLS, 2019b). We also include in this definition individuals working in jobs that do not fully use their skills, that have little room for career advancement, or that provide intermittent employment. In short, they are individuals who seek greater earnings, steeper earnings trajectories, more-stable work, or some combination of these factors.

Discouraged workers (current population survey): Persons not in the labor force who want and are available for a job and who have looked for work some time in the past 12 months (or since the end of their last job if they held one within the past 12 months) but are not currently looking because they believe there are no jobs available or there are none for which they would qualify.

1.4. Analytic Approach: Logic Model of the Program and Evaluation Strategy

Logic models (Rossi, Lipsey, and Freeman, 2004) are used to identify the rationale behind a program and provide some boundaries on what is considered part of the initiative's structure (Riemer and Bickman, 2011; Wholey, Hatry, and Newcomer, 2010). These models illustrate how program resources, activities, services, and the direct products of services (inputs and outputs) are designed to produce short-term (proximal) outcomes, medium-term (distal) outcomes, and long-term community impacts (Knowlton and Phillips, 2012).

Figure 1.1 presents the logic model underlying the intervention, illustrating how the training program is hypothesized to produce positive change for jobseekers, screening organizations, AM and energy employers, the government, and the system as a whole. The logic model guides our evaluation: Specifically, the implementation analysis explores the extent to which the inputs, activities, and outputs illustrated in the logic model were in place and how they changed throughout the course of the project. The outcome analysis delves deeply into the ways in which the program met the desired outcomes for job seekers, employers, the government, and local systems, and provides a cost-benefit analysis.

The implementation analysis tracks the following three components of the logic model:

- The **inputs** are the resources and investments that are made available to fund the project's core activities, such as money and staff to develop the curriculum.
- The **activities** include screening and recruitment of participants and establishing partnerships between government, training institutions, and employers for the development of curriculum, and the provision of training and relevant jobs.

Figure 1.1
Logic Model

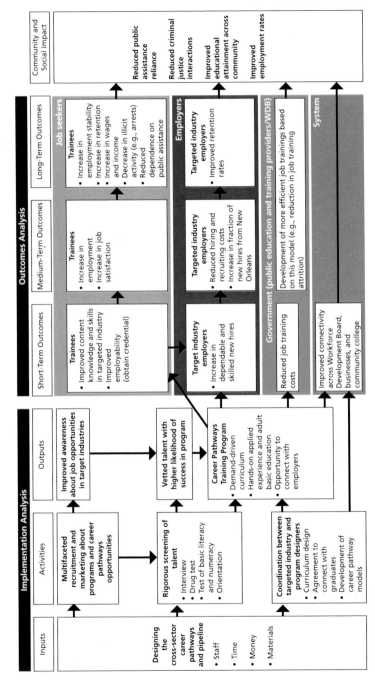

- The **outputs** are what is produced and the direct results of the activities, such as the curriculum, training, and participants' connections with employers.

Similarly, the outcomes analysis examines the short-, medium-, and long-term outcomes for job seekers who participated in the program, industry, and the government.

- The **short-term outcomes** are the hypothesized effect of the outputs, while the **medium-term outcomes** and **long-term outcomes** include expected outcomes resulting from the intervention over time.

Outcomes for participating jobseekers: We expect that workers who receive workforce training will develop more technical skills related to the industry (short-term outcomes), resulting in more job opportunities (medium-term outcomes), which lead to better jobs and improved wages (long-term outcomes). We also expect reduction in public assistance payments and reduction in criminal justice interactions (e.g., arrests).

Outcomes for industry: We expect that firms within the targeted industries will benefit from the pipeline. For the firms receiving the newly trained workers, outcomes include lower hiring and recruitment costs (short-term outcome), an increase in the fraction of new hires from New Orleans (medium-term outcomes), and, in the long term, improved retention rates for new employees (new workers should be better trained, more interested, and more likely to want to stay in New Orleans).

Outcomes for government: We expect substantial systemic gains to the government through improved efficiency in service delivery. There will be reduced job training costs because training will be given to prescreened individuals who have higher probabilities of success (short-term outcome). We also hypothesize that job training programs will become more efficient by making the curriculum client- and demand-driven through employer interviews to target needed skill gaps. The efficiency of the job training programs will be compared with other job training. For longer-term outcomes we hypothesize that there will also be lower costs to public assistance programs and unemployment programs through decreased payments and interaction as individuals move into the labor force and out of unemployment and underemployment. This would also lead to higher tax revenue for the government. Additionally, a lower number of arrests would mean less money spent on the criminal justice system, including the police department, court system, and incarceration facilities, not to mention the benefits for the potential victims of the crimes.

Outcomes for local systems: Finally, we hypothesize that the intervention will affect short-term effects on the local system, such as an increase in cooperation and collaboration among the local Workforce Development Board (WDB) (the mayor of New Orleans' OWD), the local business alliance and other nongovernmental organizations, the training providers (including a local community college) and the region's businesses. While these links already exist, we hypothesize that this program could strengthen communication and interaction, potentially yielding future programs and interventions with greater ease.

The logic model also includes broad **community and social impacts**. These are a multitude of indirect region-wide improvements that one might expect from this program: improved connectivity across the WDB, business leaders, and training providers; reduced costs associated with public assistance; and others. Note that it is outside the scope of the evaluation to analyze the impact on these broader outcomes: It is too early to determine whether these societal and community indicators have changed.

The relationships posited in the logic model are, of course, somewhat more complex than illustrated. These changes take place within a community, which may both affect and respond to the changes that the low-skill labor market or the target industry firms might experience. External factors, outside of the control of this project, could affect these processes and outcomes and therefore will be considered in an evaluation. These could include, for example, state education funding or economic shocks to New Orleans or the United States.

The above discussion focuses on desired outputs and outcomes, but it must be recognized that there is no guarantee that all impact will be positive. For example, unsuccessful training programs can waste public and private resources in the form of tax dollars, participants' time, and other resources that could be put to better use elsewhere. On a less-tangible note, unsuccessful programs can lead to unmet expectations, which can negatively affect future choices by participants and policymakers. Our quantitative estimation methods and qualitative inquiries allow for such unintended consequences. Although positive impact estimates are more encouraging, negative findings can be very informative when designing future programs.

1.5. Research Questions

Our research questions for the evaluation are based on the logic model presented in Figure 1.1. We define a research question and the related analysis as either confirmatory or exploratory. *Confirmatory analysis* seeks to confirm or disprove hypotheses; that is, to do inference on causality. Therefore, confirmatory analyses in this report will be those with the strongest identification of the causal relationship that is also connected to the underlying theories of action occurring through the program. *Exploratory analysis* is used to generate hypotheses rather than test them and offers a guide to future research. All the following research questions are exploratory unless explicitly labeled as confirmatory. In this report, we address the following research questions (the section in which the question is addressed is also listed with each question).[1]

---

[1] In our original evaluation design report, we included a research question to implement a quasi-experimental design alongside the RCT. The quasi-experimental design would have looked at recipients of job training in New Orleans that did not go through this program and thus were not screened, and compared the gains in job training for the unscreened population with our screened population. Unfortunately, we were unable to secure data for these comparisons because of privacy regulations, and did not feel comfortable claiming that any differences in training outcomes for a matched population in another state receiving different job services were due to whether or not they were screened. As such, we have omitted this intended research question from this study.

1.5.1. Implementation Study

1. How closely do the programs' features and policies follow the original plan, and how are they functioning? (Chapter 3.1)
    a. What are the programs' features and processes? To what extent do the features incorporate the best evidence-based practices to train unemployed and underemployed workers? How are these features expected to work together? (Chapter 3.1)
    b. To what extent are key stakeholders (i.e., employers, community college representatives, OWD staff) implementing the program features and process as intended? (Chapter 3.1)
    c. What are facilitators and barriers to implementing the program as originally designed? (Chapter 3.1)
    d. Have there been any unexpected consequences (either positive or negative) from how the program has been implemented? (Chapter 3.1)

2. In what ways are participants (both the trainees and employers who hire the trainees) experiencing the program? (Chapter 3.2)
    a. What are some positive and negative experiences, and how is program effectiveness perceived? (Chapter 3.2)
    b. What are participants' suggestions for improvement? (Chapter 3.2)

3. What is the nature of the partnership among the various organizations? (Chapter 3.3)
    a. What is the perceived effectiveness of the partnership among the involved entities (e.g., OWD, community college, local businesses) in establishing the Career Pathways program? (Chapter 3.3)
    b. Are there areas in which the collaboration could be strengthened? (Chapter 3.3)
    c. Are there any unintended consequences as a result of this partnership? (Chapter 3.3)

1.5.2. Outcomes Study

4. What are the levels of program participation?
   a. At what rates do individuals invited to participate in training attend training, complete training, and earn credentials? (Chapter 4.1)
   b. How do these rates vary by age, gender, baseline employment status, and baseline earnings? (Chapter 4.1)
   c. Do these rates change from the beginning to the end of the study? (Chapter 4.1)

5. What effect does the program have on employment and earnings?
   a. Confirmatory Analysis: Does offering demand-driven prescreened job training lead to an improvement in employment status following the training period? (Chapter 4.2.1)
   b. Confirmatory Analysis: Does offering demand-driven prescreened job training lead to an improvement in earnings following the training period? (Chapter 4.2.1)
   c. How do the effects of the program vary by pathway (AM, health care, and IT)? (Chapter 4.2.2)
   d. Confirmatory Analysis: How do those results differ by age, gender, baseline employment status, and baseline earnings? (Chapter 4.2.3)
   e. Are trainees more likely to get jobs in the target industry of their training pathway? (Chapter 4.2.4)

6. What effect does the program have on other outcomes?
   a. Confirmatory Analysis: Does offering demand-driven prescreened job training lead to longer job persistence? (Chapter 4.3.1)
   b. Is offering demand-driven prescreened job training related to higher job satisfaction? (Chapter 4.3.2)
   c. Confirmatory Analysis: Does offering demand-driven prescreened job training lead to fewer arrests? (Chapter 4.3.3)

7. Do higher prescreening scores relate to improvement in the training completion rate and job placement rates, wages, and employment duration? (Chapter 4.4)
8. Do a trainee's classmates in the training cohort have an impact on the success of the trainee in terms of employment and earnings? (Chapter 4.5)

1.5.3. Cost-Benefit Study

9. What is the cost per individual completing the program? (Chapter 5.1)
10. What is the value of the benefits of the program to the trainee, the government, and society? (Chapter 5.2)
11. What are the resulting cost-benefit net values of the program, including the internal rate of return (IRR) and returns on investment (ROIs), and how many years does it take for benefits to exceed costs? (Chapter 5.3)

1.6. Structure of Report

This report is structured as follows. Chapter Two discusses data sources and collection methods. Chapter Three presents the implementation analysis, answering research questions 1 through 3. Chapter Four discusses the outcomes analysis, answering research questions 4 through 8. Chapter Five contains the cost study and answers research questions 9 through 11. Chapter Six has a discussion of findings, and Chapter Seven contains a conclusion. The methodologies for each chapter are contained in the appendixes that follow. A separate appendix contains the survey instruments for the report.

CHAPTER TWO
Data Sources and Collection Methods

This project draws on both quantitative and qualitative sources of data to conduct an implementation study, the outcomes evaluation, and the cost-effectiveness study. Table 2.1 summarizes the data sources, associated population, measures used in the outcomes analysis, and whether the data source is used in the cost-benefit study. Table 2.2 presents a list of each training cohort, characteristics of the cohort, and which outcome analysis it is included in (based on data availability, while excluding the pilot cohort given it was not randomized).

2.1. Data Sources for Implementation Analysis

The implementation analysis relied on three sources of data: (1) observations of design planning meetings and review of relevant documents, (2) semistructured interviews with key stakeholders and partners, and (3) focus group discussions with trainees.

2.1.1. Observations of Design Planning Meetings and Document Review

In the first year of the project (2015), stakeholders were designing and planning the Career Pathways program prior to the program's launch. In July 2015, we reviewed the program design, curriculum, and training documents, and observed discussion sessions and meetings that OWD convened with community partners (e.g., youth training programs, Social Aid and Pleasure Clubs, and Mardi Gras Indians, all discussed later), human resource representatives and key leaders in the

Table 2.1
Sources of Data and Population Under Study

Data Source	Populations	Measures	Used in Cost-Benefit Study
Implementation Study			
Observations of design planning meetings	OWD, training providers, HR representatives, and key leaders in targeted industries		
Focus groups	Program participants		
Semistructured Interviews	Training provider instructors and program designers, employers in targeted industries		X
Program documentation	(Not applicable)		X
Outcomes Evaluation			
Program records	Program participants	Attendance, completion, whether credential was obtained	X
State administrative employment and earnings records	Program participants, control group persons	Earnings, employment status, employment duration, industry of employment	X
Telephone surveys	Program participants, control group persons	Job satisfaction	
Criminal justice records	Program participants, control group persons	Arrests	X

NOTE: HR = human resources.

Table 2.2
List of Training Cohorts

Training Start Date	Pathway	Area	Training Provider	Cohort	# Treated	# Control	Attend, Complete, Credential	Employed, Earnings, Job Stability	Job Satisfaction	Arrests
8/22/16	Advanced mfg.	Electrical	Delgado	Pilot	32					
10/31/16	Advanced mfg.	Electrical	Delgado	AM1	17	16	X	X	X	X
12/6/16	IT	IT	New Horizons	IT1	22	20	X	X	X	X
2/6/17	Advanced mfg.	Electrical	Delgado	AM3	24	23	X	X	X	X
2/7/17	Advanced mfg.	Electrical	Delgado	AM2	21	20	X	X	X	X
2/21/17	IT	IT	New Horizons	IT2	29	29	X	X	X	X
3/26/17	IT	IT	New Horizons	IT3	18	17	X	X	X	X
4/17/17	Advanced mfg.	Electrical	Delgado	AM4	23	23	X	X	X	X
8/28/17	Advanced mfg.	Electrical	Delgado	AM5	13	12	X	X	X	X
9/11/17	Health care	Patient access rep.	Ochsner	PatAcess1	20	20	X	X	X	X
9/21/17	IT	Information technology	New Horizons	IT4	4	4	X	X	X	X

Table 2.2—Continued

Training Start Date	Pathway	Area	Training Provider	Cohort	# Treated	# Control	Cohort Used for Analysis			
							Attend, Complete, Credential	Employed, Earnings, Job Stability	Job Satisfaction	Arrests
10/23/17	IT	Information technology	Delgado	CISCO1	11	10	X	X	X	X
11/13/17	Health care	Medical billing and coding	Goodwill	MB&C1	14	14	X	X	X	X
1/29/18	Advanced mfg.	Welding	Delgado	AM6	11	8	X	X	X	X
2/19/18	Health care	Medical billing and coding	Goodwill	MB&C2	10	9	X			X
2/19/18	IT	IT	Goodwill	Broadband Tech1	5	4	X	X		X
4/2/18	Advanced mfg.	Electrical	Delgado	AM7	8	8	X	X		X
5/7/18	Health care	Medical billing and coding	Goodwill	MB&C3	13	12	X		X	X
5/25/18	IT	IT	Spark	JAVA-SCRIPT1	3	3	X		X	X
6/25/18	Health care	Medical billing and coding	Goodwill	MB&C4	10	9	X		X	X

Table 2.2—Continued

Training Start Date	Pathway	Area	Training Provider	Cohort	# Treated	# Control	Cohort Used for Analysis			
							Attend, Complete, Credential	Employed, Earnings, Job Stability	Job Satisfaction	Arrests
7/16/18	Advanced mfg.	Pipefitting	Delgado	AM8	6	6	X		X	X
8/20/18	Lineman training	Lineman	Delgado	Lineman1	4	4	X		X	X
8/27/18	IT	IT	Delgado	CISCO2	7	5	X			X
8/31/18	IT	IT	Spark	JAVA-SCRIPT2	2	2	X		X	X
9/5/18	Health care	Pharmacy tech.		ptech1	4	3	X		X	X
Total assigned to training group in analysis sample					299					
Total assigned to training group, veterans					36					
Total assigned to training group in pilot					32					
Total assigned to training group					367					

NOTE: mfg. = manufacturing; rep. = representative; tech. = technician. As explained below, the total number of study identification numbers (IDs) is greater than the number of individuals because individuals randomized to the control group in a given cohort could enter the randomization pool for a subsequent cohort. Veterans that applied for training were automatically accepted in accordance with DOL regulations and thus were omitted from the outcomes analysis. Job satisfaction is drawn from the telephone surveys, and cohorts are marked as not included when we were not able to interview anyone from that cohort. New Horizons is New Horizons Computer Learning Center. Delgado is Delgado Community College. Ochsner is Ochsner Health System.

AM and energy sectors (target industries at program outset), and curriculum and training program developers. The information gathered in these discussions was used to understand the rationale behind key program components. We tracked key pieces of information, such as

- which core occupations were in highest demand and could be filled by graduates of a focused training program
- what key content knowledge, behavioral competencies, and hands-on skills and abilities would be required for those jobs in the sectors
- what facilities and materials that students would need in order to be appropriately trained
- what the obstacles or barriers for program success were that would need to be considered in the program's design
- any facilitating conditions that could be leveraged.

2.1.2. In-Depth Interviews with Program Designers, Implementers, and Employers

With support from team members at Scroggins Consulting, LLC, and Topp Knotch Personnel Inc.–– minority- and women-owned businesses located in Louisiana and subcontracted to help with data collection––we collected qualitative data to examine the implementation of the Career Pathways program. Our data collectors worked with Scroggins and Topp Knotch to conduct semistructured interviews and focus groups with the involved parties of the Career Pathways program at three points in time: November 15 through November 18, 2016; May 22 through May 26, 2017; and March 27 through April 9, 2019. Table 2.3 lists the organizations and interviewees' positions for each period. Further details on the organization partnerships are detailed in Chapter Three.

We collected information from a wide range of stakeholders involved in the design and implementation of Career Pathways, including the OWD and other city government agencies working in coordination with OWD, training providers, employers, and recipients of the trainings. In the next few paragraphs, we summarize the types of organizations and individuals included in the interviews.

Program designers and managers of the training providers: Data collectors interviewed stakeholders involved in the design of the training program. These included key staff from OWD, training providers (including Delgado Community College and New Horizons), and employers in the targeted industries. We asked about the goals and design of the training program, roles and involvement of the various organizations in designing and developing the program, the nature of collaboration among organizations, and program activities and consequences. During each data collection window, we obtained budget and cost information from the training providers and OWD.

Trainers and instructors: We interviewed trainers and instructors at the selected training provider to collect information on their experiences with the program, hindrances to implementation of the program as designed, attendance rates of participants, lessons learned to inform improvement in subsequent training sessions (this question was asked in data collection windows 1 and 2 only).

Screening and nonprofit organizations: We interviewed the organizations responsible for screening the eligibility of participants, cultural partners, ResCare, and JOB1 Business and Career Solutions (OWD's community- and industry-facing organization), to obtain information about their roles in the program and criteria used for the screening and selection process.

Employers: We interviewed the participating industry partners regarding their roles and involvement in the development of the program and training curriculum, their process for hiring training graduates, and their assessment of the skills and performance of the training graduates in the workplace (more information on employer interviews is provided in the outcomes evaluation section).

Data collectors tried to speak with at least one person in each stakeholder group organization in each data collection window. Partner organizations involved in the program changed through the project because of the modifications the program underwent throughout the course of the project. A description of these organizations and these modifications are provided in detail in Chapter Three.

Table 2.3
Stakeholders Who Participated in Interviews

Stakeholder Group	Organization	Interviewee
Data Collection Window 1: November 15–18, 2016		
Program designer	Office of Workforce Development (OWD)	• Program manager • Industry lead for infrastructure sector • Cultural partner liaison
Training provider and instructor	Delgado Community College	• Interim director of community and economic development • Navigator • Instructor
Screening organization	ResCare (Contracted operator by OWD for its JOB1 Business and Career Solutions Center)	• Career services team lead • Career advisor • Career advisor
	Social Aid and Pleasure Clubs; Mardi Gras Indians (cultural partners)	• Two cultural partner organization leaders
Industry/ employer partner	Ochsner Health Systems	• Director of workforce development
Data Collection Window 2: May 22-26, 2017		
Program designer	Office of Workforce Development (OWD)	• Program manager • Industry lead for infrastructure sector
	City of New Orleans	• Industry lead for technology sector • Director of information technology and innovation

Table 2.3—Continued

Stakeholder Group	Organization	Interviewee
Training provider and instructor	Delgado Community College	• Two instructors
	New Horizons Computer Learning Center	• Manager of admission • Manager of student affairs • Collections coordinator • Senior director for career development and operations • Training manager • Director of career services • Director of training
Screening organization	ResCare	• Career services team lead • Career advisor
Industry/ employer partner	Ochsner Health Systems	• Vice president of technology, chief technology officer
	Laitram	• Director of corporate operations
Data Collection Window 3: March 27–April 8, 2019		
Program designer	Office of Workforce Development (OWD)	• Program manager • Project supervisor
	City of New Orleans	• Executive assistant to the mayor's office • Education manager
Training provider and instructor	Delgado Community College	• Instructor • Assistant director of enrollment
Screening organization	ResCare	• Career services supervisor
Industry/ employer partner	JOB1 Business and Career Solutions Center	• WIF case manager • WIF data specialist
	Ochsner Health Systems	• Talent management director
	LCMC	• Learning and organizational development consultant
	Jericho Housing	• Executive director

2.1.3. Focus Groups with Program Participants (Trainees)

Alongside Scroggins and Topp Knotch, we conducted 32 focus groups, each with trainees from one of the training cohorts (three in data collection window 1, 17 in data collection window 2, and 12 in data collection window 3). All trainees who completed each training program cohort were invited to participate via email and telephone. Focus groups were scheduled to occur in the evening, and data collectors provided refreshments to participants, as well as gift cards as a gesture of appreciation. Invitees were offered a number of dates to attend the focus groups in each data collection window. Focus groups were arranged to hold between six and ten participants. Each focus group had between one and eight attendees, due to no-shows on the date of the focus group. In total, 116 trainees participated in the focus groups. The purpose of the focus groups was to gain a better understanding of the perceived utility of the training program, to find out in what ways participants' lives had changed (or not) since completing the program and being employed in a new career, and to gather participants' insights on how to improve the program.

We developed a set of interview and focus group protocols to gather information about the implementation of the Career Pathways program. Our protocols sought to obtain data on the implementation of the three innovative areas of the proposed program design, including the use of recruitment and screening tactics to select students into the training, training that included basic education and sector-specific skills, and the development of partnerships between government and nongovernment entities surrounding the Career Pathways program. Understanding how the training program components were implemented provides context for explaining its outcomes. This also generated knowledge and lessons learned regarding promising practices on how to develop well-functioning and sustainable partnerships that deliver quality services. To cover these topics, but also allow for new features to emerge, we used semistructured interviews that included open-ended questions with supplemental probes to examine specific topics. The protocols differed for each type of interviewee. For example, we asked partners about the nature of collaboration, their views of the pipeline, the activities in which they were involved, and how things changed. In the focus groups, we allowed for open discussion among training participants about the structure of the training, their views about its quality, and its relevance to workforce preparation.

2.2. Data Sources for Outcomes Analysis

We acquired data from several sources for the outcomes analysis.

1. **RAND baseline surveys:** At the orientation meetings, where individuals signed the consent forms for participation in the study, they also filled out a baseline survey. The survey asked about birth date, gender, current employment status, income in the prior year, and race and ethnicity. These data are used for stratified randomization and as covariates in the outcome regressions.

2. **OWD program data:** OWD provided us with information on the individuals who were part of the program (both treatment and control). Specifically, we received information on individuals' screening scores, where available, for three profiling tools: the interview, TABE, and Wonderlic. One or more of the three tool scores were missing for many individuals, either because they were not interviewed or administered the assessment (e.g., the interview scores were introduced after the first set of cohorts), or because of data loss or lack of retention of the scores. Table 2.4 lists the profiling tools investigated in the outcomes analysis; the Louisiana Workforce Commission (LWC)–based tools were never used by OWD but are investigated as potential alternatives in the analysis.

3. **LWC employment and earnings data:** We requested and received data from LWC. The data contained individual records on quarterly earnings and industry by employer. There is a two-quarter delay in which the information could be acquired from LWC, and considering the time required to process and analyze each wave of data, this report utilized data from the third quarter of 2014 through the third quarter of 2018.

Table 2.4
Summary of Profiling Tools

Profiling Tool	Description	Data source
Average pre-employment	Proportion of quarters employed in the range of 2.5 years to 0.5 years prior to randomization	Authors' manipulation of LWC data
Average pre-earnings	Average quarterly earnings in the range of 2.5 years to 0.5 years prior to randomization	Authors' manipulation of LWC data
Maximum job tenure	Maximum number of consecutive quarters in the range of 2.5 years to 0.5 years prior to randomization	Authors' manipulation of LWC data
TABE	Test of Adult Basic Education	OWD
Wonderlic	Wonderlic Personnel Test	OWD
Interview score	JOB1 screening interview score	OWD

4. **Training attendance and completion records:** We obtained individual-level data on training attendance and completion for the trainings, as well as whether the individual received a credential from the training.

5. **Telephone surveys:** We surveyed training program participants and nonparticipants to collect data not available in the administrative records. The survey allowed us to collect richer information on demographics (e.g., marital status, number of children), preprogram labor market experiences (e.g., earnings, work experience, employment and unemployment spells, turnover, and industry for at least three years before the program), job satisfaction, and experiences in the program. The data collection timeline spanned March 2018 through March 2019. We attempted to survey each participant and nonparticipant at least once after training was completed (or would have been completed). We attempted a second follow-up survey for partici-

pants and nonparticipants who were in training programs that started in 2016 and 2017.

6. **Criminal justice records:** We collected data from the New Orleans Police Department (NOPD) on each arrest by NOPD for each person across their entire life. This data was collected through April 25, 2019.

2.3. Data Sources for Cost Analysis

We used the information collected from multiple sources, including those used in the implementation and outcomes analysis. Program costs are largely based on program office budget documents collected solely for the cost analysis. For the cost analysis, we also conducted interviews with program administrators, training providers, and key HR representatives and industry leaders to obtain additional context on expenditures to more precisely measure the costs of the program. To estimate program benefits, we rely on the outcomes analysis for estimated effects on earnings. To estimate other benefits, such as fringe benefits, taxes, and government transfers, we rely on earnings data gathered for the outcomes analysis and publicly available information on eligibility requirements for public assistance programs. The details regarding data sources and methodologies are contained in Appendix C.

## CHAPTER THREE

Implementation Analysis

The implementation analysis examines whether the Career Pathways program's inputs, activities, and outputs match the logic model in Chapter Two. We attempt to understand how the program was implemented, as well as deviations from the program's original design and we note, where relevant, how the departures might have altered outcomes and impacts from those that were intended.

We conducted a qualitative analysis of the evolution and implementation of the Career Pathways program. This allowed us to capture the complexity of the program as it unfolded. Specifically, we examined how the various partners implemented the program, the extent to which it was implemented as initially proposed, the structural and logistical challenges that stakeholders faced, and how they overcame those challenges.

This implementation analysis answers three research questions, as outlined in Chapter One. These questions are regarding the implementation fidelity and functioning, the trainee and trainer experiences, and the nature of the program partnerships. This chapter evaluates each in turn. The methodology for this chapter is discussed in Appendix A.

3.1. Implementation Fidelity and Functioning

We first investigate research question 1: *How closely do the program's features and policies follow the original plan, and how are they functioning?* This includes evaluation of the following research subquestions:

    a. What are the programs' features and processes? To what extent do the features incorporate best evidence-based practices to train unemployed and underemployed workers? How are these features expected to work together?

    b. To what extent are key stakeholders (i.e., employers, community college representatives, and OWD staff) implementing the program features and process as intended?

    c. What are facilitators and barriers to implementing the program as originally designed?

    d. Have there been any unexpected consequences (either positive or negative) to how the program has been implemented?

We summarize comments from interviewees to describe the Career Pathways program as intended, and the modifications that occurred throughout the project.

3.1.1. Original Design of the Career Pathways Program

In this section, we describe the intended design of the program, its various components, and how those components were intended to work with one other (research subquestion 1a). The cross-sector job pipeline proposed by OWD was intended to be responsive to the misalignment between job preparation and labor-market needs in New Orleans. The original design of the Career Pathways training program had three innovative features: (1) using businesses and community organizations (e.g., Social Aid and Pleasure Clubs, youth employment nonprofits) to recruit and prescreen workers for training, (2) offering high-quality training that incorporates adult basic education with skills training, and (3) development of partnerships between government and non-government entities to improve outcomes for workers and employers, including creating a demand-driven curriculum. Specifically, the intervention differed from existing programs in New Orleans by incorporating a full cross-sector pipeline. Screening prior to pipeline entry would identify candidates with a high likelihood of program completion and for whom the training would lead to subsequent labor market success. The demand-driven curriculum and connections with employers would improve the probability that there would be appropriate jobs at the end of the pipeline.

In the following sections, we summarize the features of the Career Pathways program, as originally designed.

Originally planned screened recruitment: A primary objective of the pipeline is to access a population of jobseekers who have the potential to succeed in both training and subsequent work situations. OWD proposed recruiting job-seekers from the hospitality and leisure sector because many underemployed people in New Orleans work in that sector. The local hospitality and leisure sector experiences lower labor demand during the tourism offseason (summer); many workers are laid off for months during that time. While this sector is a strong supporter of New Orleans' economy, its workers are often characterized as having low skills and earning very low wages. OWD also proposed having the partners from this sector, such as local businesses and community-based cultural organizations (also considered part of this sector by the city of New Orleans) prescreen job seekers based on their ability and likelihood to succeed in the training program. This prescreening process was proposed because the aforementioned organizations are highly engaged with the target population through their missions, community-based activities and (in some instances) employing individuals from this population.

Partners from the hospitality and leisure sector consisted of community organizations, nonprofit organizations that provide youth preparation and training, and businesses. These organizations were selected because they are well positioned to identify workers with skillsets that would fit well with the Career Pathways program. The community-based cultural organizations identified were Mardi Gras Indians and Social Aid and Pleasure Clubs. The Mardi Gras Indians, who make up over 50 tribes, engage the youth generation and teach them about tribal customs and traditions, lead sewing classes each week, hold regular parading practices, and provide young members with opportunities to perform at events (Mardi Gras New Orleans, undated). New Orleans' Social Aid and Pleasure Clubs are representatives of their communities and were formed to help dues-paying members defray health care costs, funeral expenses, and other financial hardships. The number of members in these clubs range from under ten to 85 for neighborhood clubs, and several hundred for larger clubs. OWD selected these organizations because they place great emphasis on younger generations and offer opportunities for young people to carry on traditions, learn valuable skills, and perform at public and private functions across the city. While neither the original proposal from OWD to DOL nor the request for proposals made explicit mention of these cultural partners, OWD told us that the cultural partners were always considered part of the intended partnerships for recruitment and screening.

The intention was that such organizations, through their existing connections to the community, would have a sense of which candidates were most likely to succeed in the training and could therefore provide OWD with referrals—and, in the case of the cultural organizations, provide a prescreening. Though each of these categories of potential referral and prescreening organizations have different types of knowledge about potential participants' readiness to take advantage of the training program, the organizations are in a position to have observed individuals' persistence, basic literacy and numeracy, ability to take direction, reliability, and other characteristics that have been identified by training and industry representatives as critical for success in training and subsequent employment. The cultural organizations were also viewed as having interests aligned with the goals of the program; that is, they had an interest in their unemployed and underemployed members and employees receiving training and advancing their careers. The hope was that hospitality and leisure businesses, which might be reluctant to send their higher-quality workers to receive training in other industries, might be incentivized to recognize that their high-turnover industry would benefit, and that higher-quality workers would be attracted to work in the sector, even for seasonal or temporary pass-through jobs, because they would be interested in obtaining free training through the Career Pathways program.

Originally planned training: OWD originally proposed recruiting 180 candidates each year, half of whom would be selected through a randomization process to enter the cost-free training program. Training was proposed to occur in the summer because of the lull in the hospitality and leisure sector at that time. Given that the focus was to provide training in AM and energy sectors, OWD proposed partnering with Delgado for the training, as it had for other training programs prior to the Career Pathways program. The proposed training was expected to represent a coordinated effort between Delgado and hiring firms in the AM and energy sectors to develop curricula designed to teach technical skills for which employers had current needs. The proposed duration of the training program was eight weeks, with courses taking place four hours a day, five days a week. After conferring with Delgado and employers, OWD proposed implementing four specializations or *career pathways* related to AM and energy, including welding, electrical, pipefitting, and industrial maintenance.

The AM and energy trainings were designed to have two parts, or "stackable credits." The first part—CORE Plus—taught math and basic skills and used the National Center for Construction Education and Research (NCCER) curriculum. The second part taught participants NCCER entry-level skills specific to each specialization or career pathway of their choosing. The proposed training was designed to provide opportunities for participants to obtain stackable credentials as they progressed. When participants completed CORE Plus and passed the qualifying tests, trainees had the opportunity to obtain a NCCER CORE certificate of completion and Occupational Health and Safety Administration (OSHA) 10 certification.[1] As they continued with the specialization component, participants could obtain a NCCER level-1 certificate of completion in that specialization (e.g., electrical level-1). Some students might opt to participate in higher levels of specialization (such as level-2 certificates within the specialization they select and accumulating credentials over time), but these activities would be outside of the program under evaluation.

Originally planned partnerships between government and nongovernment entities: Another feature of the Career Pathways program was to have government and nongovernment entities partner with one another to develop the program and ensure successful out-

---

[1] An OSHA 10 certification signifies that the recipient has taken a 10-hour course on occupational safety and health for construction workers and is able to recognize, avoid, abate, and prevent safety and health hazards in the workplace.

comes for participants, including completion of training and securing jobs that pay sustainable wages. To reach that end, it was proposed that OWD would cultivate partnerships with employers surrounding three main activities: developing the training curriculum, introducing training graduates to potential hiring firms through job fairs or site visits to potential industry partners, and providing graduates with on-the-job training opportunities. The goal was for these industry partners to be more likely to employ trainees, especially due to the prescreening component and employer-coordinated training curriculum.

3.1.2. Implementation of the Career Pathways Program Through Time

We now describe how each of the three main components of the Career Pathways program was implemented and highlight areas in which OWD and its partners modified their approaches from the proposed design. We also describe barriers to implementation and any unintended consequences (research subquestions 1b, 1c and 1d). A timeline of key modifications made to the proposed program design is located in Chapter 1 of the separate online-only appendix to this report.

Implemented screened recruitment: The population to be targeted by the New Orleans Career Pathways program changed from what was proposed in 2014. As indicated previously, in the original proposal, OWD planned to recruit training candidates primarily from the hospitality and leisure sector, both from community organizations and businesses. The goal was to target the unemployed and underemployed populations in that sector and receive referrals from partners in that sector based on their experiences employing or otherwise working with prospective candidates. Cultural partners were also considered to provide recruitment and screening. OWD invited organizations from the hospitality sector early on in the program design phase to discuss collaboration and recruitment.

There were two separate program design sessions held: The first was for representatives from nonprofit organizations that provide youth preparation and training through structured employment programs and for representatives from local businesses in the hospitality and leisure sector; the second was for individuals representing the cultural organizations. However, organizations in the previously mentioned design session were particularly resistant to partnering with OWD on this initiative because they did not want to lose their best employees. In addition, due to issues related to political tensions between city government and major hospitality employers in New Orleans at the time, the partnerships with this segment of the hospitality and leisure sector never came to fruition as originally planned, forcing the OWD to reevaluate its target population and focus. The intended partnership with local nonprofit and for-profit businesses in hospitality and leisure therefore dissolved prior to implementation of the program.

As a next step, in the spring of 2016, OWD decided to rely exclusively on cultural partners to help with recruitment and screening. Specifically, the cultural partners—Social Aid and Pleasure Clubs and Mardi Gras Indians—were expected to help with recruitment by referring people into the pipeline from their respective membership bases and communities—and, in addition, to conduct the prescreening of potential participants.

In the initial planning stages, there were numerous cultural organizations that expressed interest in partnering with OWD and had representation at the Career Pathways program design session for Social Aid and Pleasure Clubs and Mardi Grad Indians, which the OWD held in 2015. The cultural organizations were interested in partnering because they saw the value of the pipeline in improving the livelihoods of those in their communities. The cultural organizations had discussions regarding the roles they could play and how they could assist with the recruitment and prescreening of potential participants. However, OWD experienced significant challenges in formalizing partnerships with the majority of the cultural organizations. According to the OWD, the primary reasons for this were related to limited capacity of some cultural organizations to take on program roles and responsibilities, requesting an amount of financial compensation for their time and involvement that OWD could not satisfy, or both. Subsequently, only two cultural organizations formally partnered with OWD for the Career Pathways program. These two organizations were compensated for their involvement using WIF grant funds; however, as described later, the role of the cultural partners evolved over the implementation of the program.

Recruitment of trainees: In 2016, the two cultural partners advertised the program to members of their organizations and in their communities. However, this role was taken away from them for subsequent cohorts, because the marketing approaches they used had limited reach and impact, and did not lead to the sufficient number of recruited individuals needed for the summer program. This is not surprising, given that only two organizations were given the responsibility to recruit a large number of potential participants. The result was that the two cohorts that began in 2016 were partially recruited using the cultural partners, whereas all subsequent cohorts did not use recruitment from the cultural partners—reflecting one of a few changes around this same point in time that were later determined to have had a significant impact on the effectiveness of the training programs.

OWD organized a series of information sessions around the city in spring 2016, to which the cultural partners were to send their referrals to be prescreened. During these information sessions, the cultural partners disseminated the information they were given by OWD regarding the training and support that was to be provided.

Prior to the information sessions, OWD briefed the cultural partners about the structure of the program and where the trainings would occur to prepare them for their participation in the information sessions, prescreening, and referral processes. The cultural partners' participants were paired with OWD (JOB1) team members who helped them with recruiting participants. However, the cultural partners reported being unprepared to answer some potential questions regarding the training. According to OWD, there were certain complex details about the training and services that the cultural partners were not expected to have answers for and that required input from OWD. For example, participant access to transportation or other supportive services is not as simple as a yes or no answer and often requires added context about eligibility requirements. To the extent possible, the nuances of the program were shared with cultural partners in a manner that minimized the sharing of incomplete information.

The cultural partners also indicated that they would have liked to contribute to defining the goals and the design of the training program and have been aware of what the training curriculum consisted of, so they could be more convincing when discussing the benefits of the program and overcome participants' mistrust and disbelief about the program.

As indicated above, the recruitment efforts of the cultural partners were ultimately inadequate to ensure high turnout at the events or overall interest in the Career Pathways program. In 2016, after months of recruitment, only 32 potential participants were recruited, compared with the 180 participants originally proposed by OWD. As a result, in fall 2016, OWD opened recruitment to the public and turned to ResCare—a contractor for OWD, responsible for supporting the Career Pathways program in all its stages—to be the primary recruiter of candidates. The cultural partners were still involved in recruitment at this time, but this ended by early 2017. An outreach position to market the program was created through ResCare. The opportunity to be considered for entry into the program was made available to the public. Modified means of marketing and recruitment strategies included

1. social media (Twitter, Facebook)
2. radio advertisements
3. posting advertisements on Craigslist (community forum)
4. holding informational meetings at community centers
5. providing information about the program in the city's five Opportunity Centers, where tablets were present for easy candidate sign-up
6. using available data to reach out to previous users of OWD services.

In addition, OWD asked other city agencies to promote and market the Career Pathways program through their industry liaisons.

Opening recruitment to the public led to changes in the targeted population. While the initial proposed design targeted underemployed individuals from the hospitality and leisure sector, the changes in marketing strategies opened it up to the general public, including those who were unemployed as well as gainfully employed in other sectors but seeking a career change or increase in salary.

Prescreening: Given that cultural partners were unable to make enough referrals to meet recruitment numbers, which led to recruitment opening up to the general public, the partners' role in prescreening shifted. OWD asked the cultural partners to prescreen all those who had applied to the training during the informational session that all applicants were required to attend. The cultural partners were tasked with using 15 questions, covering six core competency areas, to determine their eligibility to move forward in the recruitment process. OWD provided these questions to the cultural partners. This prescreening protocol is in Chapter Two of the separate, online appendix. The questions covered topics related to interest and willingness to participate, attendance, and timeliness.

After this first wave of prescreening, OWD felt that the cultural partners were uncomfortable asking the prescreening questions and determining participant eligibility—particularly of individuals the cultural partners did not directly know but who were from the partners' communities. This might have affected the quality of partners' screening abilities and led to the screening being less selective. It was the opinion of OWD that, at least in some cases, the screening was in no way selective, and that the cultural partners were recommending any interested persons for training. In addition, cultural partner prescreeners reported difficulty in getting through all of the questions that were provided by OWD.

Given this, as well as the fact that the cultural partners were having difficulty recruiting, OWD made the decision to transition prescreening responsibility to another entity; AM1 and IT1 were the only cohorts in the analysis under the prior screening through cultural partners, whereas later cohorts had the new screening process. OWD had conversations with the Opportunity Centers, established by the Network of Economic Opportunity, to assist in screening individuals interested in the Career Pathways program. The five Opportunity Centers in New Orleans are traditional workforce development agencies that have the capacity to assess workforce readiness skills and have their own detailed standard screening to determine eligibility. However, the five Opportunity Centers expressed concern about selecting participants using a lottery process rather than providing services for all eligible applicants. Although the five Opportunity Centers used the same procedure to identify eligible participants, OWD was concerned that that the Centers would not adhere to the requirement of the RCT and decided to take on the screening responsibility itself, with support from ResCare, at the end of 2016.

OWD began using its own screening process to determine eligibility to enter randomization for the training program. This screening system was utilized for all cohorts recruited after the "pilot cohort" through the end of the project. Screening during this time was implemented over a two-day candidate orientation. On the first day, candidates received information about eligibility to enroll in the program, details about the training itself and the various career pathways available, and potential employment opportunities that could be open to participants after successful completion of the training. On the second day, candidates who remained interested and eligible to continue brought in their required documentation, completed paperwork, and were then interviewed by an OWD or ResCare staff member. The following documents made up the aforementioned components of this screening (full documents are in the separate appendix):

1. **A Career Pathways Program Interest form:** This document consists of basic questions, such as candidate contact information and career pathway interest area.
2. **Checklist for Career Pathways Program Interest form:** This document consists of questions that aid in determining whether candidates meet the basic eligibility requirements for the program and could provide the necessary documentation needed to enroll, such as the individual's Social Security card and three most recent pay stubs.
3. **Member Triage form:** This document consists of questions that further delve into candidate eligibility (e.g., if one had a criminal background). In addition, this document aided OWD and

ResCare staff in identifying whether candidates were already enrolled in or would need of any type of assistance.

4. **Orientation interview questions:** Interviews consisted of ten questions that fell under six domains and measured such competencies as communication skills, initiative, and fluency with technology.

Following the two-day orientation sessions, members of the OWD and ResCare team who screened candidates met as a group to debrief and discuss their opinions about which candidates should continue on to be entered into the randomization pool. According to OWD and ResCare team members, common reasons for candidates to not pass the screening round included having a negative attitude or displaying rude behavior.

As OWD was utilizing this screening process, it sought to improve the suitability determination system to make it more comprehensive and objective while still having the ability to identify individuals most suited for the training program (not just those who were eligible). OWD contracted Cygnet Associates to work on a new, more detailed screening system that was composed of criteria to measure candidate suitability for the training program and individual career pathways. The updated screening system assesses candidates' career goals, persistence, satisfaction with status quo, level of social supports, circumstances, and optimism to change (see Appendix D for new suitability determination system materials, which were adopted by OWD in August 2017).

The final screening process was designed to evaluate whether candidates were a strong fit for training and the career pathways, as well as their likelihood to succeed in future employment opportunities in sector specializations. Similar to the "interim" screening process that OWD used before this new system was put into place, interested individuals were required to visit the OWD office to attend a two-day orientation and obtain an application packet. Interested individuals were asked to complete the application and provide OWD/ResCare staff with documentation (e.g., Social Security card, pay stubs) to determine initial eligibility. Candidates were also required to provide a resume and were given "homework" after day one of the orientation. In some cases, this consisted of writing a career plan—demonstrating reasons why the individual wanted to apply to the Career Pathways program and particular specialization, as well as how this person would leverage their new skillsets to progress professionally. Individuals were also asked to complete a personal budget, which OWD used to identify if candidates needed or qualified for any support services that would enhance their likelihood to succeed in the training (e.g., child support, transportation needs).

In addition, the new candidate suitability determination system also assessed if individuals could make the time commitment to be successful in and after the training program. On day two of the orientation, individuals who made it through the first phase of screening were invited back for an interview by OWD and ResCare staff. The interview took about 45 minutes. The interviewer used a scoring rubric to obtain an overall score of suitability. The OWD/ResCare team no longer met as a group to subjectively discuss candidate eligibility. Based on the scoring rubric, individuals who underwent the screening interview and received a score of 70 or higher were deemed eligible for the program and placed into the randomization pool, despite any opinions the screening team might have had regarding candidates' suitability—this is the greatest differentiating factor between the two screening processes.

In addition to the abovementioned screening processes, interested individuals who applied to the Career Pathways program in 2016, 2017, and 2018 were also screened for literacy, numeracy, and other basic skills using the TABE or Wonderlic Cognitive Ability Test.[2] This information was used differently depending on the individual career pathways. For AM, for example, academic readiness screening was used to inform the training itself regarding the level of math and literacy that should be addressed. Interested participants were not denied participation if they scored low. On the other hand, for the IT path-

---

[2] The Wonderlic Cognitive Ability Test (formerly known as the Wonderlic Personnel Test) is a popular group intelligence test used to assess the aptitude of prospective employees for learning and problem-solving in a range of occupations.

way, the academic readiness information was used as one of the suitability and eligibility criteria.

The intent of the modification of the recruitment strategies was to improve participants' selection process to ensure participants completed the program. These changes coincide with the increased effectiveness of the training programs, including program completion for the cohorts recruited after 2016, as discussed in Chapter Four.

While program designers initially proposed recruiting 180 training candidates to enter randomization once each program year (totaling a training cohort of 90 participants), given the challenges in recruitment, OWD changed its procedures so that recruitment occurred multiple times in each program year and on an ad hoc basis, with smaller cohorts. Training also occurred multiple times throughout each program year. Instead of three cohorts with 90 trainees each, there were ultimately 24 cohorts of varying size.

Those participants recruited in summer 2016 were the recruits who were prescreened by the cultural partners, referred to as the *pilot cohort*. Given the far smaller numbers recruited than anticipated and the realized need to change recruitment methods—and in consultation with the technical advisory support from the WIF National Evaluation Coordinator (Abt Associates) and DOL—this cohort was not randomized. All were entered into treatment and therefore were not part of the outcomes analysis RCT sample. This cohort was the only trainee group provided with the opportunity to receive funding to obtain a NCCER electrical level-2 certification, because of circumstances related to their pilot status.

Implementation of training: We next discuss the how the training component of the program changed over time. As explained earlier in this chapter, initially, OWD and its partners proposed recruiting participants into four career specializations related to AM and energy, based on market trends, but this was not accomplished. Participants were only recruited into the electrical specialization because of the small number of participants and their interest. However, in November 2016, the career pathway expanded to include training in IT, when labor demand in the energy sector did not grow as predicted due to falling oil prices. Many businesses in AM and energy, which were initially interested in partnering with the Career Pathways program, backed out of participating.

Expanding the pathway training into IT also aligned with the Mayor's Office of Economic Development's strategic planning around expanding certain industry areas in the city—IT being one of those priority sectors. The Employment and Training Administration of DOL chose the city as a member of its TechHire Community of Practice, in which TechHire grantees share resources and successful practices to support jobseekers in technology occupations. New Orleans created a mirror position for IT, similar to the Infrastructure Sector Lead position (funded by the WIF grant) whose role was to identify job projections and assess sectoral needs; however, that position was not funded by the grant. In September 2017, OWD again expanded its pathways to include health care as a way to meet local labor market demands and the needs of the largest health care systems in Louisiana.

Throughout the remainder of this section, we will at times reference Table 3.1, which contains the counts of individuals at each level of training, by pathway.

AM and energy: Between summer 2016 and spring 2018, a total of 262 individuals were recruited and consented to participate across the pilot cohort (who did not go through the randomization process) and the nine subsequent cohorts (who did go through randomization)

Table 3.1
Counts of Trainees, Attendees, Completers, and Credential Acquirers

	AM	IT	Health Care	Total
Consented	262	220	134	616
Assigned training	173	124	70	367
Attended training 1	133	103	70	306
Completed training 1	99	83	57	239
Attended training 2	47	16	2	65
Completed training 2	42	5	1	48
Acquired credential	96	67	40	203

NOTE: Numbers include training participants who were veterans or from the pilot cohort, none of whom are part of the outcomes analysis.

for training in AM with specializations in electrical, welding, pipefitting, and lineman skills.

Delgado provided all of the training in the AM pathway. The start dates are provided in Table 2.1. Delgado also leveraged its own internal services regarding special needs and adult education to support training participants. According to OWD, the training curriculum had been developed by both Delgado and AM and energy sector businesses through a DOL Trade Adjustment Assistance Community College and Career Training grant. According to OWD, Delgado convened instructors and employers to design the curriculum. Our interviews with employers indicate that they provided general suggestions regarding the curriculum. Overall, the curriculum was broad and based on NCCER standards. The industry partners strongly recommended to the community college that it add an OSHA10 course to the training to improve the competitive edge of pathway graduates when they seek jobs; this recommendation was accepted. In April 2017, Delgado also added a Green Infrastructure curriculum component to the training, which was first initiated during the fourth cohort's CORE Plus module. This latest addition was motivated by the city's emphasis on initiatives surrounding waste and water management and coastal restoration and resiliency.

The typical duration of the AM training program was six to eight weeks long, with courses taking place four hours a day, five days a week. The length of the training also varied depending on whether it included Green Infrastructure. The training had two components: a core component (CORE Plus) and an NCCER electrical level-1 component. The core component taught math and industry occupation safety. It included nine math modules that the students needed to pass before moving on (if they chose) to electrical level-1. Students were allowed to retest in math if they did not pass a module the first time. In electrical level-1, students were taught entry-level skills related to electrical work and were provided with opportunities to apply the tools in their classes.

During the training, students were tested in order to obtain their NCCER CORE certificate of completion, as well as their OSHA10 credential. As of spring 2018, cohorts also had the opportunity to be tested to receive a certificate of completion in Green Infrastructure. There had been a lapse period between the Core Plus and the electrical level-1 components of the training for cohorts 1 and 2, due to low registration numbers following CORE Plus. Subsequently, trainees from those cohorts who were interested in moving on to the next training module were forced to wait until the electrical level-1 course for cohort 3 was offered (April 2017). This led to a number of participants dropping out because they needed to find employment for financial reasons. As indicated above, because of the decrease in the number of participants, the three cohorts were grouped together to receive electrical level-1 training.

Of the 173 assigned training in AM, 133 attended at least one class. Of those, 99 completed the first round of training, and 96 acquired credentials. Also notably, 42 of the 47 individuals who began the second round of training also completed it.

IT: Between fall 2016 and spring 2018, a total of 220 individuals across nine cohorts consented to participate in IT training, and 124 trainees were selected to begin training in this career pathway. Of the 124 trainees, 103 have completed training, with 67 receiving a credential. The rate of participation in the second round of training was much lower in IT than in AM, with only 16 individuals beginning second-round IT training, and only four completing it.

New Horizons Computer Learning Center (New Horizons), Delgado Community College, Operation Sparks, and Goodwill provided the IT trainings. New Horizons Computer Learning Centers, one of the largest IT training companies in the United States, trained four of the nine cohorts from fall 2016 through the end of summer 2017. In 2017, OWD asked Delgado to provide two new cohorts with Cisco training starting in October 2017, and then again in August 2018. Similarly, OWD brought in Goodwill to provide IT training for one cohort in February 2018, and Operation Sparks to provide training to two cohorts in JavaScript starting in April and July 2018.

OWD indicated that it had used New Horizons before for other trainings not related to the WIF grant. For the IT pathway, New Horizons implemented a curriculum that it had used in other trainings. Employers were not asked to provide input regarding the curriculum.

The IT pathway curriculum focused on Network+ and Security+ cer-tifications.[3] After completing the curriculum, New Horizons offered testing for certification purposes. All the classes were fully online. Students could therefore attend from any location, though they were encouraged to attend one or two sessions per week from one of the New Horizons Learning Centers in New Orleans. The sessions were recorded so that students could either attend them live or access them after the lecture. The duration of the training varied for these cohorts, as trainees were provided with a range of start and end dates to choose from for their coursework. On average, training took place for five days a week, and lasted four and half hours per day. The course included a lab where students practiced answering test questions. There were no opportunities for students to have hands-on experiences with IT employers.

The students enrolled in New Horizons' IT pathway did not have the academic preparation that traditional students have, so New Hori-zons made several minor adjustments to the training (free of cost to OWD), including placing more emphasis on fundamental concepts in the curriculum, providing online study sessions for the participants (cohort 2), requiring certificate testing to occur within 30 days after curriculum completion, and allowing participants to take the certifi-cation test more than once. Because of the online nature of the train-ing, New Horizons incorporated approaches to engage students during the classes, such as polling and opportunities to communicate with the instructors during breaks or specific periods. But even with those techniques, there were issues with student attendance. New Horizons, as well as OWD, indicated that attendance was not consistent. Purely online courses presented a challenge in keeping students motivated and engaged in their courses. Students required more support in both mastering the content and managing their time. This mode of teach-ing and learning did not allow for face-to-face interaction between faculty and students. Faculty were therefore unable to detect student

---

[3]   Network+ is an entry-level certification used to measure skills as a network technician. Security+ is an entry-level, vendor-neutral security certification that builds off of the net-work security knowledge covered by the Network+ certification.

lack of engagement and intervene in a timely manner. New Horizons and OWD engaged in a variety of efforts to monitor and encourage attendance. For example, New Horizons monitored every trainee who logged into the sessions. For those who did not, faculty members would contact them via e-mail and telephone. New Horizons also provided attendance lists to OWD so they could follow up as well.

Health care: Between fall 2017 and spring 2018, a total of 134 individuals consented to be randomized for training in health care programs. 70 were assigned training; all 70 attended the first round of training and 57 completed it. Participation in the second round of training was rare, with only two individuals starting and one completing. 40 of the trainees acquired credentials (Table 3.1). For five cohorts, one-on-one patient access training was provided by Ochsner Health Systems, while the remaining four trainings on medical billing and coding were provided by Goodwill. Ochsner's training program trained participants in entry-level administrative and clinical positions but offered stackable credentials for participants to pursue further education in the health care field.

Because the health care trainings were built and taught later than the trainings for AM and IT, we were only able to capture information from a smaller window of implementation time. Details on impediments to trainings and experiences of trainees are therefore limited.

The expansion of the training programs to cover sectors with high job demand increased the alignment between training programs and labor market needs, which might have contributed to the positive employment outcomes seen with the IT and health care cohorts, which we discuss in Chapter 4.

Development of partnership between government and nongovernment entities: During the proposal preparation and initial planning, OWD worked jointly with businesses to develop the vision of the New Orleans Career Pathway. According to OWD, the businesses have moved away from this partnership for a variety of reasons, including lack of capacity, inadequate funding for continued participation, or perceived misalignment of their mission with the mission of the Pathway.

While employers, as part of WIF, engaged in coordinated activities with OWD, their partnership with the OWD can be described as "loosely coupled." Our interviews with a few employers indicated that their involvement mostly consisted of orientation-session presentations to participants about job opportunities and skills needed at employers' firms, and the sectors they serve. In 2017, a few employers had been invited by OWD to conduct mock interviews with Pathway candidates to train them on how to answer questions during job interviews. Two employers reported reviewing the resumes of a few Pathway candidates for positions that they had posted. One of them committed to hiring one Pathway graduate. The two employers interviewed indicated that there was no guarantee they would hire the candidates. In fact, employers stated that they relied on other labor force pathways to access qualified workers.

Throughout the duration of the program, however, OWD reported that they were strategic in terms of which businesses they would formally invite into a partnership. An example of one such business was Ochsner Health Systems. In 2019, Ochsner was among the top five employers in the Greater New Orleans area in terms of number of employees, and it had been involved in other workforce development programs. One such program consisted of customized training for entry-level positions on "the clinic side of the house." More than 290 individuals were trained, and about 250 of those trainees received employment at Ochsner facilities after completion of the program. OWD replicated this type of training with Ochsner using WIF funding. The training targeted entry-level positions in medical assistance, and was specific to Ochsner's needs.

3.2. Trainee and Trainer Experiences

We next evaluate research question 2: *In what ways are participants (both the trainees and employers who hire the trainees) experiencing the program?* This includes evaluation of the following research subquestions:

    a.   What are some positive and negative experiences, and how is program effectiveness perceived?

b.   What are participants' suggestions for improvement?

To answer these questions, we summarize comments from inter-viewees, focus group participants, and responses from the phone survey regarding stakeholders' experiences in the program and its perceived quality and effectiveness in meeting its goals.

3.2.1. Stakeholders Noted a Number of Positive Aspects About the Training Program

First, trainees in focus groups reported that the curriculum provided a "good foundation" of the basic fundamentals to the sector. Trainees who had completed the pipefitters training noted that they appreci-ated how the instructor stressed the importance of safety, given how important this knowledge was for obtaining and retaining a job in the energy or construction industries. One focus group participant com-mented that he still studies the safety book provided in the course, and that "the safety tips were excellent advice." Trainees were often realistic about what the courses provided. For example, one focus group par-ticipant in a pipefitters course noted, "I would refer individuals to the program but will explain to future students not to expect to become experts from just this course. In order to become an expert in this field, they will have to attend additional training." And about 75 percent of phone survey respondents either "strongly agreed" or "agreed" to the prompt: "The trainer balanced lecture with hands-on activities in the field."

Second, the WIF program offered counseling and social supports as a way to support students' attention and their retention in the pro-grams and to encourage course completion. For example, as part of the WIF grant, participants were connected to OWD navigators or case managers who helped students develop a personal strategy based on their needs. The navigators also provided reactive advisement when needed. The navigators would talk with struggling students and pro-vide them with needed support. Participants in the AM cohort were also connected to career developers at Delgado to help them identify available jobs and prepare their resumes. This service was part of other funding sources that Delgado was able to use for this program. A Del-

gado staff member explained the various ways that the college supported the students in the program:

> Academically, I have pulled each student into my office and cre-
> ated a resume for every one of the students for all 60 students. Even
> if they already had one, we made an updated one that included all
> of the certifications that they would receive through the program
> and putting Delgado on [the resume] as well. Also, I helped with
> role-playing interviews and practicing standard questions that are
> typically asked during a job interview. Each student also works
> with a teacher who talks with students about their long-term aca-
> demic goals, such as whether the student would want to continue
> their education at Delgado for an associate degree; the teacher
> could help them do that and transfer credits.

New Horizons also incorporated some support to help participants develop their resumes. New Horizons initially did not have the
capacity to provide this support, but as part of the WIF grant, its staff
were trained on helping participants develop their resumes by the IT
lead for the city of New Orleans. In addition, in 2017, the cultural
partners started to provide mentorship services to all participants in
the AM and energy and IT pathways. Their role had transitioned from
prescreening and recruiting participants to supporting and monitor-
ing them. The cultural partners convened quarterly events where they
addressed a topic relevant to the participants. Cultural partners sup-
plemented the quarterly meetings with biweekly check-ins with participants to discuss personal issues or challenges they were facing that
could affect their completion of the pathways.

Third, when asked about the quality of pathway program trainees
compared with other employees in similar jobs at the business, interviewees noted anecdotal evidence and their personal observations that
the program trainees were of a higher quality: Trainees had stronger
content knowledge when they started and seemed to know what to
expect while on the job, which then led to higher retention rates.

3.2.2. Areas in Need of Improvement

More opportunities for hands-on practice or real work experience: Across all cohorts, the trainees with whom we spoke reported that the program did not provide them with enough real work experience. They viewed the pathway as helping them obtain accreditation for entry-level positions but lacking adequate opportunities for participants to apply what they learned in labs or real settings. Participants reported the need to be provided with internships to build work experience and to be competitive in the labor market. The most vocal students were those in the electrical and pipefitters' courses, who noted that having more time doing hands-on practice while in the course would have been beneficial. As one pipefitting student put it:

> Most of the training occurred in class with the book and we only spent two hours of shop work. I noticed that plenty of students could not relate to what they learned in the book to the actual tools in the shop. . . . hands-on, many students were clueless and their practical skill was a minimum.

An electrical trainee commented:

> We need additional time in the shop to do actual projects. This skill level will not prepare me in getting a job unless I get employed as an apprentice.

This perspective was partially corroborated in the phone surveys. A medical billing respondent reported in an open-ended comment: "Training is a good idea on medical billing, but it did not go deep enough and there wasn't any guidance on applying it or finding a job." However, as noted above, 75 percent of the respondents agreed or strongly agreed that the trainer balanced lectures with hands-on activities in the field.

Lack of awareness and communication about stipends or other benefits available to students: Participants were provided with a materials and transportation support to ensure they attended their classes. For example, pipefitters and electricians were provided with tools and equipment. However, this was communicated haphazardly to students, and trainees did not know what types of benefits or supports were available to them. For example, in one focus group, a participant relayed a story that a student transferred from another location and told the participant about a stipend the participant might qualify for that he was not aware of. The participant was also told that all equipment and tools would be provided but then got charged for boots. This focus group participant expressed frustration about not receiving exact information about stipends, materials, or benefits he could have utilized. He commented: "The program needs to provide all the information to students prior to the course starting date, and give all the tools/ supplies the first day of class."

Although some monetary and material support was offered, a common concern among focus group participants and interviewees was that such support was inadequate. In some cohorts, participants were not allowed to work while enrolled in the training; however, according to our employment records, many did. While being a full-time student could make participants focus on their training, this setup also made them financially vulnerable. Training provider interviewees reported that some students dropped out because they took on a job to provide for their families.

Personalized instruction and curriculum that integrate employability skills: We heard from all focus groups a desire for the course to be extended so that trainees could learn more and be more employable on the job market. One phone survey respondent's open-ended statement supported this perspective: "It's difficult to find a job because the training is only level 1 and job opportunities want higher level." Training providers also commented that the courses were meant to be entry-level by design and were to whet the appetite of trainees— if they wanted more education, they could do that. And yet, it was understood that an entry-level course might be inadequate. One training provider interviewee commented:

> I think the only hindrance is the time constraint. You can get through a level one of training within the time allotted but you cannot get into a level two. Level one gives you that entry-level introduction to the craft but it does not give you that deep dive

that you would have in a level two. The funding portion is great; we just need more of an extended period on the amount of time that the training must be completed in. That would really just be the best service to the students.

Another common theme was the lack of flexibility in the curriculum and instruction, noting that there was little individualized instruction. For example, one focus group participant noted that he would recommend changing the curriculum so it would not to be "so strict." Another trainee added: "Personalize the curriculum and allow the instructor more leeway to come up with their own course curriculum and get it approved by the program director." A course instructor also noted that the curricula were intended to meet industry standards so that students could pass a credential test; given the pace that was expected of the instructor, it was difficult to personalize learning for struggling students.

Moreover, the content of the curriculum focused on knowledge and applied skills (to some extent), but not on workplace competencies or employability skills, such as showing up every day on time, following instructions, or problem-solving—all of which are important skills to have for any job. Stakeholders we interviewed, including employers, indicated a need for the training to integrate the development of soft skills. One employer stressed that, for entry-level jobs, it is more important to ensure that the participants have the soft skills needed, such as interviewing skills, dependability, and punctuality, than having the technical skills because employees can always learn technical skills on the job. Faculty conducting the training also indicated the need for the training to promote those nontechnical employability skills but voiced challenges in doing so, given that the participants "are adults and likely to have been set in their ways."

Reported lack of job counseling and employer engagement: More than half of surveyed training participants reported receiving information on job opportunities from OWD through JOB1, compared with a third of nonparticipants (see Figure 3.1). Similarly, about 40 percent of surveyed participants received resume development and job-readiness services from JOB1, compared with 30 percent and 23 per-

Figure 3.1
Survey Responses to Supports that Program Participants Received from OWD, JOB1, or Opportunity Centers

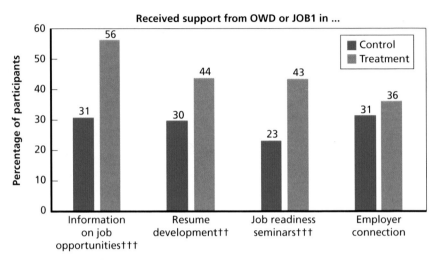

SOURCE: Telephone surveys of project participants (treatment and control).
NOTE: Nonresponse weights used, described in Appendix B. For the difference between the treatment and control group, ††† indicates p-values smaller than 0.01; †† indicates p-values smaller than 0.05; † indicates p-values smaller than 0.1.

cent of nonparticipants, respectively. While the non-WIF grant JOB1 services were made available to the nonparticipants (control group of the project), the services did not facilitate participant-employer connections, despite this being a key intended feature of the Career Pathways pipeline. Less than a third of training participants and nonparticipants reported OWD or JOB1 introducing them to employers, with the difference between treatment and control groups for this question being not statistically significant.

The survey finding is substantiated by findings from the focus groups. A majority of focus group participants commented that they would have liked more connections with employers.

In 2016 and 2017 data collection windows, some participants reported that not many businesses came to their classes to talk about job opportunities and the ones that did were unrelated to their field.

No focus group participants in 2019 recall an employer coming to a classroom to talk about jobs available or what it was like to work for a particular employer. Though the training program providers and the JOB1 Career Center provided job counseling opportunities, there was not an opportunity embedded in the course for students to engage with employers. Rather, students could attend job fairs or talk with a job counselor. One focus group participant noted: "As long you visit the JOB1 office on a regular basis, they are willing to assist you." Focus group participants suggested that program designers "reach out to more companies to assure student get internships or permanent jobs."

Phone survey respondents had mixed responses on whether the training was useful in helping them find a job. Of the spring 2019 wave of phone interview responses, 49 percent responded that they strongly disagreed or disagreed that the training they received was helpful in finding a job, and 51 percent strongly agreed or agreed; 48 percent agreed or strongly agreed that it helped them find a *better paid* job. There is also mixed evidence about the extent to which the training helped them in their current job, with 55 percent agreeing or strongly agreeing that it helped them succeed in their current job and 51 percent agreeing or strongly agreeing that it helped them advance in their job. See Appendix B for the full results on these survey questions.

One phone survey respondent in a health care industry cohort noted:

> The biggest problem was that the promise for internships were not fulfilled. The internships were promised in the orientation.

Another health care cohort phone survey respondent stated:

> It felt like they were just trying to meet a quota rather than truly help the students be successful. It didn't feel like they really helped students find jobs or connect with the industry.

An AM cohort phone survey respondent painted a dismal portrait of employment support:

JOB1 gave me the runaround. No follow-ups and no leads. They have not been any help or assistance at all. My caseworker doesn't contact me. Nobody follows up with me.

Screen to include a person's comfort level with certain tasks: Employers and instructors with whom we spoke commented that, on a few occasions, they had encountered talented trainees who simply were not prepared for the challenging nature of the job once they completed the program. As an example, one instructor commented that it would benefit the program to incorporate a screening and application process before the students start training as a way to determine people's comfort levels and awareness of the expectations of the jobs. He explained:

> I've run into people who are uncomfortable doing things such as climbing a ladder and things you need to do on the job. If [training providers] had a physical test [that participants had to pass] to be able to be qualify to go into the program, . . . an applicant would demonstrate they are comfortable doing the task or [the applicant is] not going to be necessarily employable.

3.3. Nature of the Program Partnerships

In this section, we evaluate research question 3: *What is the nature of the partnership among the various organizations?* This includes evaluation of the following research subquestions:

a. What is the perceived effectiveness of the partnership among the involved entities (e.g., OWD, community college, local businesses) in establishing the Career Pathways program?
b. Are there areas in which the collaboration could be strengthened?
c. Are there any unintended consequences as a result of this partnership?

We summarize comments from interviewees to document ways in which stakeholder organizations partnered, how those partnerships changed over the course of the project, and note interviewees' responses about ways in which the collaborations could be strengthened.

The "loosely coupled" dynamic among the stakeholder partners described throughout this chapter resulted in some challenges. As detailed in Chapter 3.1, OWD made a number of changes in partners over the course of the project. Two of the most dramatic changes were in which organizations would undertake the recruitment and screening of applicants and which industry partners would be invited to participate.

- Cultural organizations were transitioned out of the role to recruit and prescreen potential applicants to the program into more of a mentorship role; OWD asked ResCare to take over the task of recruiting and screening potential trainees.
- When confronted with the challenge that industry partners in the energy sector would no longer participate, OWD shifted the career pathway from energy and AM to AM and IT, and then added health care.

We found that some partners did not have the capacity to implement certain aspects of the program successfully. For example, the cultural partners that were selected to help recruit and prescreen the potential candidates did not have sufficient experience for prescreening and felt uncomfortable doing so with members from within their communities, nor did they have sufficient funding or organizational capacity to carry out the requested activities. They seemed unable to identify whether potential participants had the needed skills to complete the training. Subsequently, OWD made the decision to take on the prescreening responsibility that was originally intended for hospitality employers and then given to the cultural partners. OWD took on this responsibility to ensure that prescreening was implemented in a standardized way and would yield a sufficient number of training candidates. We also heard from interviewees that the loose coupling left them feeling less than integral to the planning and thus left out of decisionmaking.

As described in Chapter 3.1, throughout the course of the project, OWD modified programming and adjusted the components of the program, which seemed to result in more-aligned and better-functioning relationships. In our final window of data collection in 2019, we found that the organizations involved with OWD in the last year of the program had a strong sense of purpose in the partnership and reported that collaboration was positive. OWD, training providers, and employers we interviewed in this window commented that the partnerships were "strong" and "valuable." Employer interviewees, in particular, reported strong working relationships with OWD and training providers and that they felt that their employment needs were taken into consideration. Overall, there were many positive comments about the working relationships among the three stakeholders. For example, an interviewee from a training provider commented, "We all share the same goals. How are we going to help this city and the people in this demographic? Everyone has the mindset of how we are going to help. We all have a good rapport and good relationships. And we are very supportive to get people into trainings that will change their lives."

3.4. Conclusion

This chapter summarized findings from the implementation analysis to answer three research questions:

1. How closely do the program's design features and policies follow the original plan, and how are they functioning?
2. In what ways are participants (both the trainees and employers who hire the trainees) experiencing the program?
3. What is the nature of the partnership among the various organizations?

In response to research question 1, we found that OWD implemented the program components but modified the program features over the course of the project, and did so in a strategic manner based on internal determinations about whether partnerships were successful and whether the program was operating in a way that would benefit the number of trainees it was intended to. Expanding the career pathways to include IT when industry partnership with the energy sector fell through is one example of the agility with which OWD used its WIF funding to respond to workforce needs and the priorities of the Office of Economic Development and the city overall. In September 2017, OWD also expanded its pathways to include health care to meet local labor market demands and the needs of the largest health care systems in Louisiana. These shifts highlight the advantages of public-private relationships in developing demand-driven training curricula and choosing the pathways most likely to be of benefit to the local economy. In addition, ensuring consistency in screening and randomizing participants by OWD leading this process—instead of social and cultural partners and Opportunity Centers as initially proposed—seems to have led to better program assignments.

In response to research question 2, we found that stakeholders reported a number of positive impressions of the program. Trainees in focus groups reported that the curriculum provided a "good foundation" of the basic fundamentals to the sector. The WIF program offered counseling and social supports as a way to support students' attention and retention in the programs and to encourage course completion. Finally, employers with whom we spoke reported that the Career Pathways program trainees, anecdotally, had stronger content knowledge when starting a job and seemed to know what to expect while on the job, which then led to higher retention rates. We also found a number of areas that stakeholders reported were in need of improvement. Both trainees and employers wanted the training to provide more opportunities for hands-on practice or real work experience (e.g., internships or on-the-job exposure). Moreover, communication about the availability of stipends or other benefits to trainees was lacking; many trainees with whom we spoke were unaware that these were available. Trainees also noted that instruction and curriculum could be more individualized and integrate employability skills—such as showing up on time and following direction—which employers reported wanting from new hires. Job counseling and employer engagement was also reportedly lacking. An instructor also noted that the program could be improved if the screening mechanism for entrance into the program included a person's comfort level with certain tasks, since the instructor noticed that some students were not prepared for the types of uncomfortable tasks they could encounter (such as climbing a ladder).

In response to research question 3, we found that, over time, the nature of the partnerships and relationships shifted and adjusted. By the final two years of the project, OWD recognized that a loosely coupled partnership was not as effective as they had hoped. OWD decided to be more strategic in terms of which employers they invited to participate, and to guide training program development to be demand-driven specifically for those local employer partners. In making these types of midcourse corrections and creating tighter relationships among the partners, OWD succeeded in developing stronger partnerships than those with which it started and in creating a more purpose-driven program overall.

The modifications that occurred over the course of the study seemed to strengthen the program design because they were more responsive to local context and capacity. The modifications did not affect the overall design and its components, but they improved implementation. Specifically, these modifications improved the alignment of training programs with local labor market needs, improved recruitment methods, ensured better screening processes, and strengthened partnerships with employers. As noted in Chapter 3.1, these modifications, over time, might have contributed to the success of the program that we discuss in Chapter Four, in that later cohorts that experienced the modifications had better outcomes than earlier cohorts.

CHAPTER FOUR
Outcomes Analysis

Chapter Three discussed how the Career Pathway program's implementation plan and goals followed and at times differed from the implementation in practice. In this chapter, we take that implementation as given and examine the effect of the program on various outcomes. We investigate the analysis related to the quantitative analysis of the effectiveness of the program, as delineated in research questions 4 through 8. These encompass an evaluation of the program participation (research question 4); the effects on employment and earnings (research question 5); the effects on secondary characteristics of job persistence, job satisfaction, and arrests (research question 6); the relationships between profiling tool scores and outcomes (research question 7); and whether the characteristics of a trainee's peers are related to employment and earnings outcomes (research question 8).

The research design for this analysis is an RCT. This allows for straightforward statistical analysis that is not contaminated by selection bias that would affect evaluation of nonrandomized job training programs. That is, consider an alternative research design in which the sample of individuals that get training self-select into training and the comparison group does not select into it. In this case, training status might be partially the result of positive attributes of the trainee (such as drive, grit, and ability) and would also affect employment, earnings, and arrests. Without careful modeling and analysis, this selection into training would bias the results toward finding positive effects due to these related attributes. Through randomization, however, both the treatment (assigned training) and control (not assigned training) group

67

members selected into the same pool; our analysis is free of this complicating factor.

Given that randomization occurs after screening, both treatment and control persons have passed the screening threshold, and we cannot contrast outcomes for individuals who did not pass the screening within the cohort. Thus, the analysis measures the effectiveness of the demand-driven pipeline among a population of *prescreened individuals*, and not the complete effect of the training pipeline; i.e., the effectiveness of both screening populations for training *and* delivering demand-driven training with firm coordination. The details of the methodology, as well as descriptions of treatments for validity, are contained in Appendix B.

For evaluating outcomes, the unit of analysis is always the individual who enters into the training program randomization pool. We were unable to acquire data, outside of a few interviews, that would have allowed outcome analysis on the employers, such as whether they felt the training program was providing them with more-qualified candidates. For context of the magnitude of the different treatment effects, Table 4.1 presents the average of the various investigated outcomes for the control group. Because of the randomization, Table 4.1 therefore presents what average outcomes would have been for the population admitted to the program, absent the Career Pathways intervention. For example, we find that average quarterly earnings for the control group are $3,317.[1] Table 4.1 also indicates that 6.5 percent of individuals were arrested in the period after the start of training and before the end of data collection (an average of 1.5 years).[2] Because it is of particular interest in the discussion, we also provide the control group arrest rate for men. We will reference the average values shown in Table 4.1 when discussing the size of the estimated impacts of the training program.

---

[1]   All earnings in this report are expressed in real terms, as of quarter 3 of 2018, the final quarter for which we have employment and earnings data.

[2]   Given that we have exact dates of the start of training and when the data sample ended in April 2019, we calculate the fraction of year based on the number of days.

Table 4.1
Average Outcomes for Control Group After Training

Outcome	Mean	Standard Deviation
Employed (fraction)	0.663	0.473
Quarterly earnings	3,315	4,044
Job duration (quarters)†	0.496	0.340
Job satisfaction (0-3)*†	1.742	1.105
Arrested post-training (fraction)	0.065	0.247
Arrested post-training, men	0.109	0.313

NOTES: * Higher values indicate greater satisfaction. All estimates come from authors' calculations and authors' data. † = set to missing for those who were not employed after training.

4.1. Program Participation

We first turn our attention to research question 4: *What are the levels of program participation?* This includes the following research subquestions:

  a. At what rates do individuals invited to participate in training attend training, complete training, and earn credentials?
  b. How do these rates vary by age, gender, baseline employment status, and baseline earnings?
  c. Do these rates change from the beginning to the end of the study?

We next provide the results of the outcomes analysis. The first set of outcomes we look at involve program participation. For those assigned to the training group, we calculate the percentage who attended or completed the first and second round of training, as well as the percentage who acquired a credential. We calculate this separately for each quarter that individuals assigned to training groups to show trends over time. These rates are presented in Figure 4.1.

The attendance rate, defined as attending at least one class session, for the first round of training is relatively high at around 83 per-

Figure 4.1
Training Participation and Credentialing Rates by Quarter Assigned Treatment

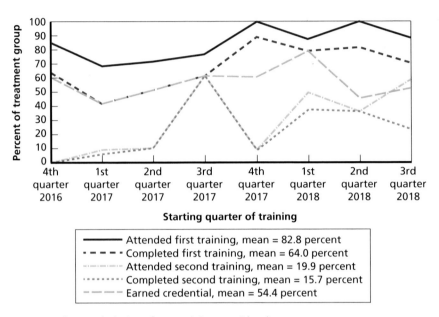

NOTE: Authors' calculations from training provider data.

cent. The attendance rate for the optional second round of training is substantially lower, at 20 percent of those assigned to training, which is 31 percent of those who completed the first round of training. Of the 83 percent who attend at least one session, 77.8 percent completed training, for an overall completion rate of 64.4 percent. This is a relatively high rate of completion for training programs aimed at disadvantaged workers who face several obstacles to participation and have a lower income to support at least partial removal from the labor market during training. The average credential rate of 54.4 percent (or 65.7 percent, conditional on attending at least one session) is relatively high as well, given that credentials could be important signals of skills to potential employers.

Finally, there is an overall upward trend in most of these measures of participation. Table 4.2 presents simple bivariate regressions

Table 4.2
Regressions of Training Participation Outcomes on Starting Year and
Quarter of Training Assignment

	Attended First Training	Completed First Training	Attended Second Training	Completed Second Training	Credential Attainment
Starting date (in years)	0.154**	0.232**	0.281**	0.188*	0.066
	(0.021)	(0.013)	(0.041)	(0.086)	(0.583)
# Obs.	261	261	261	261	261
# Study IDs	261	261	261	261	261

NOTES: Obs. = observations. This analysis is considered exploratory. Each effect is estimated in a separate regression. P-values are shown in parentheses. They are calculated using 2,499 wild bootstrap replications (null imposed). Bootstrap clusters are defined at the training cohort. Each regression additionally contains a constant. *** indicates p-value smaller than 0.01; ** indicates p-value smaller than 0.05; * indicates p-value smaller than 0.1.

of program participation outcomes on the quarter that training assignment happened (measured in years) and a constant within the treatment group only. We find positive coefficients (or improvements over time in measures of participation) that are statistically significant for all but credentialing. The coefficients are large; for example, the completed first round of training coefficient of 0.23 suggests that training cohorts that started one year later have completion rates on average 23 percentage points higher. This demonstrates that not only are the program participation outcomes relatively high for these types of job training programs and populations but they were improving significantly with later cohorts. As discussed in Chapter Three, this may be due to changes in program implementation (such as recruitment and screening methods), to the mix of pathways offered, or simply to improvement over time in the quality of the program.

In Table 4.3, we analyze the relationship between sociodemographic variables (as reported in the baseline) on the probability of attending and completing the training and obtaining credentials, among individuals randomized into training. We found that women were more likely to obtain credentials than men, and the difference

Table 4.3
Predictors of Training Attendance and Completion and Credential Attainment: Socio-Demographic Variables

	Attended	Completed	Credential
Female	0.112	0.090	0.127***
	(0.147)	(0.112)	(0.003)
Employed	0.034	0.037	0.040
	(0.471)	(0.457)	(0.442)
Income above 5k	0.047	0.105	0.121*
	(0.472)	(0.112)	(0.056)
Older (>= 35 years old)	0.102**	0.157*	0.187**
	(0.015)	(0.058)	(0.016)
# Obs.	208	208	208
# Study IDs	208	208	208

NOTES: This analysis is considered exploratory. Attendance and completion are for the first round of training. Sample includes only individuals randomized into treatment. Each reported coefficient is estimated in a separate regression. P-values are shown in parentheses. They are calculated using 2,499 wild bootstrap replications (null imposed). Bootstrap clusters are defined at the training cohort level. All regressions control for cohort fixed effects and for strata (gender, employment, income, age) fixed effects. Includes 2017 and later cohorts. *** indicates p-values smaller than 0.01; ** indicates p-values smaller than 0.05; * indicates p-values smaller than 0.1.

is relatively substantial and statistically significant (11.2 percentage points). We also found a similar higher probability of earning a credential for participants with reported incomes larger than $5,000 a year. Notably, we also found that older individuals (older than 35) have substantially higher rates (ranging from 12 percent to almost 21 percent higher) of attending and completing training and earning credentials. These differences are statistically significant, at the 0.10 level or lower.

4.2. Program Effects on Employment and Earnings

We next evaluate research question 5, *What effect does the program have on employment and earnings?* This involve several research subquestions, as described below.

4.2.1. Overall Effects of the Program on Employment and Earnings

We first examine research subquestions 5a: *Does offering demand-driven prescreened job training lead to an improvement in employment status following the training period?* and 5b: *Does offering demand-driven prescreened job training lead to an improvement in earnings following the training period?* Table 4.4 provides the estimates of the effects of the training program on participants' employment. We define employment as whether an individual has non-zero earnings in a given quarter. Our analysis includes only cohorts that ended their training at least one quarter prior to the third quarter of 2018, which is the latest quarter for which we have administrative employment and earnings records; we included in the analysis every quarter of post–training period data on employment and earnings that was available (except for the analysis represented by Figure 4.3, which will be discussed later in this chapter).[3]

The first row in Table 4.4 shows the ITT treatment effects. These results are based on treatment assignment, whether the individual assigned training ever attended training or not. Overall, pooling all cohorts, we do not find effects that are statistically different from zero. Based on the previous analysis that indicates participation was dramatically increasing in successive cohorts, and based on the assumption that there is a return to experience, or learning-by-doing, in the organization and implementation of the training programs (both for the city and for the training providers), we examined whether there was a clear break point after which training impact was dramatically better in terms of positive results on employment and earnings. The second

---

[3]   For the analysis represented by Figure 4.3, we limit the sample to individuals observed at least five quarters after the end of training, in order to estimate the trend of the effect on earnings over time.

Table 4.4
Average Effects on Employment Status

	All Cohorts	2016 Cohorts	2017 and Later Cohorts
ITT (OLS with training assignment)	−0.007	−0.285*	0.043
	(0.867)	(0.087)	(0.336)
TOT (2SLS with training attendance)	−0.009	−0.311*	0.056
	(0.867)	(0.085)	(0.329)
# Quarterly obs.	1,591	376	1,215
# Study IDs	395	59	336

NOTES: OLS = ordinary least squares; TOT = treatment on the treated; 2SLS = two-stage least squares. This analysis is considered confirmatory. Each effect is estimated in a separate regression. *P*-values are shown in parentheses. They are calculated using 2,499 wild bootstrap replications (null imposed). Bootstrap clusters are defined at the training cohort level for treated individuals and at the individual (across time) level for control individuals. Replication Wald tests are robust to bootstrap clusters and individuals participating in more than one cohort. All regressions control for cohort fixed effects and cross-strata (gender, employment, income, age) fixed effects. Employment regressions control for average employment prerandomization. Earning regressions control for average earnings prerandomization. *2016 cohorts* refers to those cohorts that began training in 2016; *2017 and later cohorts* are those that began training in 2017 or later. *** indicates significance levels smaller than 0.01; ** indicates significance levels smaller than 0.05; * indicates significance levels smaller than 0.1. Interference is adjusted using Benjamini and Hochberg's (1995) procedure, with domains defined by sample (e.g., 2016 cohorts for both ITT and TOT analysis are in one domain).

row presents the TOT effect, which is estimated using 2SLS regressions, using treatment assignment status as an instrument for attendance. This measures the effect for those who attend at least one day of the training. This makes the effects slightly larger in magnitude, given the fraction of the people that never attend is nonzero. The ITT results are the more policy-relevant of the two, because they capture the reality that treatment assignments can be made but there may always be some who do not attend despite being offered the treatment.

We also split the sample into cohorts that started in 2016 and cohorts that started in 2017 or later. In general, the effects for the first two cohorts (AM 1 and IT 1) are negative and significant, with a lower probability of employment for those assigned into the training group. This negative effect disappears and even becomes slightly positive (although not statistically significant) for the 2017 and later cohorts.

Table 4.5 presents the effects on quarterly earnings. We present the results for both unconditional earnings (values of zero entered for any person in a quarter they did not work) and conditional earnings (regressions limited to observations where there were positive earnings that quarter).[4] We again find dramatically different effects for the 2016 cohorts and the 2017 and later cohorts. For the 2016 cohorts, there is a negative effect, albeit not statistically different from zero. In comparison, we find that for the other cohorts, there is a positive and statistically significant effect on quarterly earnings. The average impact in the latter case is about $804 additional earnings per quarter in comparison with the group not randomized into training, which is an increase of almost 25 percent over the control group average of $3,317 (Table 4.1). For the TOT (the effect for attendees), the estimated average causal impact on earnings for later cohorts was $1,051 per quarter, which represents an increase of almost 30 percent over the average control group earnings in this same time period.

The treatment effects are slightly larger for the earnings conditional on employment than when earnings of all sample members (regardless of employment) were considered. This suggests that the impacts on earnings may not be driven simply by treatment group members having a higher probability of being employed, but by an effect on earnings. However, the two sets of results are very similar. Given the parameter of greater interest in the unconditional earnings (as it is the overall program effect), from here, we limit the presentation pertaining to earnings to that outcome.

---

[4] Note that the conditional earnings analysis captures both the potential shift in the sample (who is employed in the treatment and control group) and the impact on earnings. Thus, it does not fit within the experimental framework of specifically looking at the impact of quarterly earnings conditional on employment, holding constant the effect of treatment on employment.

Table 4.5
Average Effects on Earnings

	Quarterly Earnings			Quarterly Earnings (Conditional On Employment)		
	All Cohorts	2016 Cohorts	2017 and Later Cohorts	All Cohorts	2016 Cohorts	2017 and Later Cohorts
ITT (OLS with training assignment)	247.477	−2140.726	803.201**	330.810	−1241.857	903.705**
	(0.531)	(0.113)	(0.020)	(0.387)	(0.247)	(0.012)
TOT (2SLS with training attendance)	316.925	−2410.684	1050.075**	403.149	−1317.251	1109.946**
	(0.533)	(0.106)	(0.018)	(0.389)	(0.248)	(0.011)
# Quarterly obs.	1,591	376	1,215	1,072	256	816
# Study IDs	395	59	336	324	52	272

NOTES: This analysis is considered confirmatory. Each effect is estimated in a separate regression. P-values are shown in parentheses. They are calculated using 2,499 wild bootstrap replications (null imposed). Bootstrap clusters are defined at the training cohort level for treated individuals and at the individual (across time) level for control individuals. Replication Wald tests are robust to bootstrap clusters and individuals participating in more than one cohort. All regressions control for cohort fixed effects and cross-strata (gender, employment, income, age) fixed effects. Employment regressions control for average employment prerandomization. Earning regressions control for average earnings prerandomization. *2016 cohorts* refers to those cohorts that began training in 2016; *2017 and later cohorts* refers to those that begin training in 2017 or later. *** indicates significance levels smaller than 0.01; ** indicates significance levels smaller than 0.05; * indicates significance levels smaller than 0.1. Inference is adjusted using Benjamini and Hochberg's (1995) procedure, with domains defined by column of the table.

We split the sample into 2016 cohorts and 2017 and later cohorts for several reasons. First, there were fundamental shifts in the program between these years, as detailed in Chapter Three. Among these are large changes in how individuals were recruited and how they were screened. Second, there are very large differences in the effectiveness of the program across these two time periods. We can see that immediately in Table 4.4. We re-estimated a modified version of the main specification regression for quarterly earnings in which we allowed for different treatment effects before and after a given time point. We tested this for every possible division point of time to separate the sample into two periods; we also compared it with no split. The model with the best fit, as defined by having the lowest overall Bayesian Information Criterion and Akaike Information Criterion, was to split the sample right after the first two cohorts that began in the first quarter (the fourth quarter of 2016). This model fit was better than no split or any other choice of a split, suggesting that there was a shift in effectiveness after the first quarter.

We also looked at whether a particular quarter or specific quarters stand out as having an earnings impact different from earnings impacts in other quarters. Specifically, we explored differential training effects by the starting date of the training by running the same regression across all of the cohorts, but interacting treatment status, as well as pre-treatment average wage, with the quarter that the cohort started. Figure 4.2 presents these results. The only quarter with a statistically significant and negative effect is the fourth quarter of 2016 (i.e., AM 1 and IT 1).

All together, we consider these results to be evidence of a meaningful shift in the program and its effectiveness from the first two cohorts (starting in 2016) to the remaining cohorts (starting in 2017 and later), and we consider the 2017 and later cohorts to represent the fully implemented training program, which is what we are interested in evaluating. These findings also align with the period in which there were substantial changes to the recruitment and screening methods used, as discussed in Chapter Three. Specifically, recruitment shifted from a focus on community partners to a range of open recruitment methods pursued by OWD, and the screening switched from the community partners to OWD's interview profiling tool and TABE test, both happening between these two time periods. For these reasons, for the remainder of this chapter, we focus on the fully implemented program of the 2017 and later cohorts. In a few exceptions, we examined the first two cohorts as well, but, unless otherwise noted, the reader should assume that the following results apply only to the 22 cohorts that started after 2016 and not those first two cohorts in 2016.

We also examined whether the magnitude of the treatment effects changed as a function of time after training completion. The sample

Figure 4.2
ITT Effect on Quarterly Earnings for Each Quarter in Which Cohorts Started Training

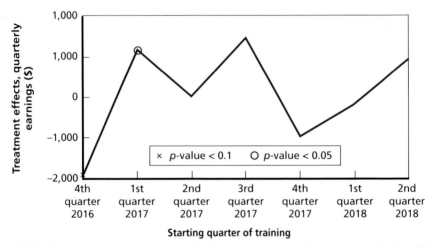

NOTES: This analysis is considered exploratory. *P*-values are calculated using 2,499 wild bootstrap replications (null imposed). Bootstrap clusters are defined at the training cohort level for treated individuals and at the individual (across time) level for control individuals. Replication Wald tests are robust to bootstrap clusters and individuals participating in more than one cohort. The regression interacts treatment status and preprogram average earnings with beginning quarter of training, and additionally controls for cohort fixed effects and cross-strata (gender, employment, income, age) fixed effects.

was limited to individuals for whom we observed at least five quarters of post–training date outcomes, so that the results are not conflated with changes in the sample (as each time point has the same individuals). We examined this question in two ways. First, Figure 4.3 presents the results from a nonlinear model, allowing a different treatment coefficient for each post-training quarter. This figure shows that there is no meaningful change in the treatment effect the longer the person has been out of training. Second, we ran a regression of quarterly earnings on the number of quarters after the end of training interacted with treatment status, as well as the other usual control variables. The coefficient on this interaction represents a linear trend in the treatment effect on earnings. The estimate is not statistically significant but is positive at around $80, suggesting a higher treatment effect per quar-

Figure 4.3
ITT and TOT Effects on Quarterly Earnings by Quarters After Training

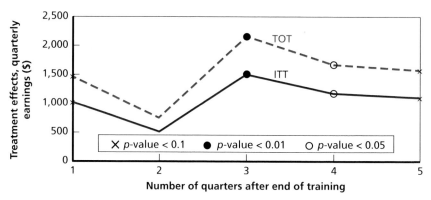

NOTE: This analysis is considered exploratory. *P*-values are calculated using 2,499 wild bootstrap replications (null imposed). Bootstrap clusters are defined at the training cohort level for treated individuals and at the individual (across time) level for control individuals. Replication Wald tests are robust to bootstrap clusters and individuals participating in more than one cohort. The regression interacts treatment status and preprogram average earnings with beginning quarter of training, and additionally controls for cohort fixed effects and cross-strata (gender, employment, income, age) fixed effects.

ter after end of training, or a $320 higher effect after a year, although again, this is not statistically different from no trend.

4.2.2. Variation of Effects of the Program on Employment and Earnings Across Pathways

We investigate research subquestion 5c: *How do the effects of the program vary by pathway (AM, health care, and IT)?* This represents a middle ground between analyzing average total effects of the initiative, as in Tables 4.4 and 4.5, and analyzing effects disaggregated by cohort. Evaluating effects by cohort could better inform what types or areas of training are more successful in moving individuals into better-paying jobs. However, the variation in results among cohorts can be driven by many factors, such as implementation differences, changes in demand from potential employers, or other random factors. Therefore it can be difficult to generalize conclusions from impact estimates from one training episode. Conversely, aggregate estimated effects offer the possibility to average out potential fluctuations in external factors that affect outcomes but provide little information on different effects by training area or pathway.

Our middle ground between the two approaches is to group cohorts by pathway and estimate average impact for each pathway separately. Figure 4.4 presents the results. It shows that the training related to health care had the most considerable returns in terms of quarterly earnings, with an estimated effect of over $1,900 per quarter. However, it is important to note that we have post-training employment and earnings data for only two cohorts that were trained in this pathway. Updating the estimates with additional quarters of post-training earnings from these and later cohorts, particularly in medical billing and coding, could result in important revisions to this average estimate.

We also find that the cohorts trained in AM had an impact on their quarterly earnings of $639, significant at the 10-percent level. This figure increases to $909 if we account for attendance. Finally, the estimates for IT are not statistically significant and are smaller, though they are still positive and have a meaningful magnitude.

4.2.3. Variation of Effects of the Program on Employment and Earnings Across Trainee Subgroups

We investigate research subquestion 5d: *How do those results differ by age, gender, baseline employment status, and baseline earnings?* We looked at effect by age, gender, self-reported employment at baseline, and self-reported earnings at baseline. Figures 4.5a and 4.5b present the results. We found large effects for participants who were female, older than 35, reported to be unemployed at baseline, and reported to earn less than $5,000 a year. The only groups for which differences are statistically different from each other are for employed versus unemployed, with those unemployed at baseline having significantly better outcomes than those employed at baseline.

Figure 4.4
Average Effects on Employment and Earnings, by Pathway

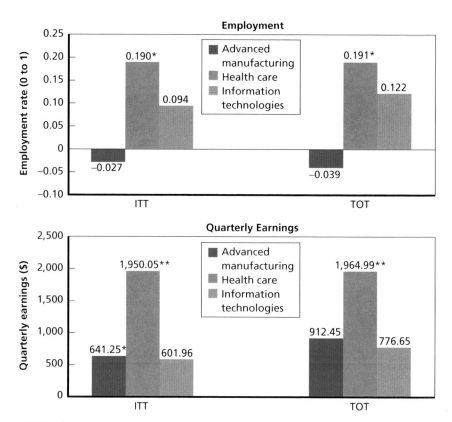

NOTES: This analysis is considered exploratory. The regressions have 1,215 observations with 336 unique Study IDs. Approximately 47 percent are in AM, 19 percent in
health care, and 34 percent in IT. Each grouping of bars is estimated in a separate
regression. P-values are shown in parentheses. They are calculated using 2,499 wild
bootstrap replications (null imposed). Bootstrap clusters are defined at the training
cohort level for treated individuals and at the individual (across time) level for control
individuals. Replication Wald tests are robust to bootstrap clusters and individuals
participating in more than one cohort. All regressions control for cohort fixed effects
and cross-strata (gender, employment, income, age) fixed effects. Employment
regressions control for average employment prerandomization. Earning regressions
control for average earnings prerandomization. Results include only 2017 and later
cohorts. *** indicates p-values smaller than 0.01; ** indicates p-values smaller than
0.05; * indicates p-values smaller than 0.1.

Figure 4.5a
Effect on Employment by Subgroups

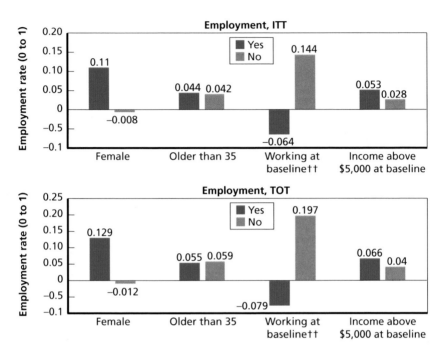

NOTES: This analysis is considered confirmatory. Each pair of effects (e.g., female and male, older and younger) for a given outcome and sample is estimated in a separate regression. P-values are shown in parentheses. They are calculated using 2,499 wild bootstrap replications (null imposed). Bootstrap clusters are defined at the training-cohort level for treated individuals and at the individual (across time) level for control individuals. Replication Wald tests are robust to bootstrap clusters and individuals participating in more than one cohort. All regressions control for cohort fixed effects and cross-strata (gender, employment, income, age) fixed effects. Employment regressions control for average employment prerandomization. Earning regressions control for average earnings prerandomization. Sample includes 2017 and later cohorts. *** indicates significance levels smaller than 0.01; ** indicates significance levels smaller than 0.05; * indicates significance levels smaller than 0.1. For the difference between groups within a category, ††† indicates p-values smaller than 0.01; †† indicates p-values smaller than 0.05; † indicates p-values smaller than 0.1. Inference is adjusted using Benjamini and Hochberg's (1995) procedure, with domains defined by outcome (employment or earnings) and separately for point estimates (does training assignment help these groups?) and for the differences (are there differences between the two categories within a group?).

Figure 4.5b
Effect on Earnings by Subgroups

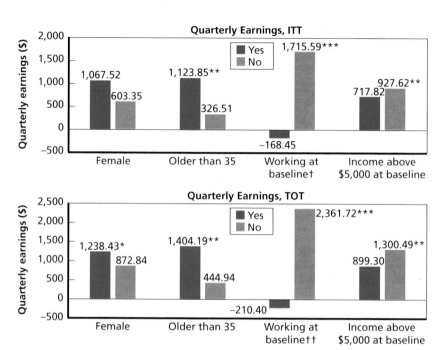

NOTES: This analysis is considered confirmatory. Each pair of effects (e.g., female and male, older and younger) for a given outcome and sample is estimated in a separate regression. P-values are shown in parentheses. They are calculated using 2,499 wild bootstrap replications (null imposed). Bootstrap clusters are defined at the training-cohort level for treated individuals and at the individual (across time) level for control individuals. Replication Wald tests are robust to bootstrap clusters and individuals participating in more than one cohort. All regressions control for cohort fixed effects and cross-strata (gender, employment, income, age) fixed effects. Employment regressions control for average employment prerandomization. Earning regressions control for average earnings prerandomization. Sample includes 2017 and later cohorts. *** indicates significance levels smaller than 0.01; ** indicates significance levels smaller than 0.05; * indicates significance levels smaller than 0.1. For the difference between groups within a category, ††† indicates p-values smaller than 0.01; †† indicates p-values smaller than 0.05; † indicates p-values smaller than 0.1. Inference is adjusted using Benjamini and Hochberg's (1995) procedure, with domains defined by outcome (employment or earnings) and separately for point estimates (does training assignment help these groups?) and for the differences (are there differences between the two categories within a group?).

4.2.4. Effectiveness of Training on Employment in Target Industry

We next look at research subquestion 5e: *Are trainees more likely to get jobs in the target industry of their training pathway?* Table 4.6 presents the results of a series of regressions, each with a dependent variable that is an indicator for working in the given target industry, regressed on treatment status (an indicator for being employed in that industry before the training period), and on fixed effects for randomization blocks and cohorts. We do this regression for all individuals as well as for subsets of those (treatment and control) in the pathways intended for the target industry in question. We find overall increases in the proportion working in health care and in IT, with the health care effect

Table 4.6
ITT Employment in Target Industries Treatment Effects

	Pathway	AM	Health Care	IT	# Obs.	# Study IDs
			Employed in			
	All	−0.003	0.100	0.009***	718	238
		(0.792)	(0.225)	(0.006)		
Randomization cohort	AM	−0.005			351	118
		(0.800)				
	Health care		0.554		107	41
			(0.210)			
	IT			0.014	260	79
				(0.118)		

NOTES: This analysis is considered exploratory. Each cell is from a separate regression. Regressions additionally control for the *p*-values, calculated using 2,499 wild bootstrap replications (null imposed). *P*-values are shown in parentheses. Bootstrap clusters are defined at the training-cohort level for treated individuals and at the individual (across time) level for control individuals. Replication Wald tests are robust to bootstrap clusters and individuals participating in more than one cohort. Each regression additionally controls for an indicator for working in the target industry baseline randomization strata characteristic (gender, binary age, baseline employment status, and binary baseline income). *** indicates *p*-values smaller than 0.01; ** indicates *p*-values smaller than 0.05; * indicates *p*-values smaller than 0.1.

being larger but not statistically significant; the effects are substantially larger when limited to the pathways intended for the target industries, although the decrease of the *p*-values from the smaller samples and far fewer cohorts in the clustering leads to nonsignificance. Meanwhile, we find no effect for treatment in increasing employment in AM industries. Health care is much more dominated by women trainees (about 97 percent of the individuals), while AM is around 86 percent male. IT is approximately even across gender. None of the other randomization strata are as disproportionately sorted between pathways outside of gender. Given the gender findings of Figures 4.5a and 4.5b, it is unclear whether the observed heterogeneity in findings reflects differential effects by pathway, gender, or both.

4.3. Program Effects on Other Outcomes

We next look at research question 6: *What effect does the program have on other outcomes?*

4.3.1. Job Persistence

We examine research subquestion 6a: *Does offering demand-driven pre-screened job training lead to longer job persistence?* We look at post–training period job stability by examining the duration of each job held after the end of the training period. The average observed job duration is about half of a year, but many periods of employment were ongoing at the end of our observation period in the third quarter of 2018. Treatment could lead to longer durations because of the ability to find better jobs, or to shorter durations because workers are able to transition out of worse jobs into better ones. Table 4.7 presents the treatment estimates from the Cox proportional hazards model. We do not find any meaningful impact of training on job duration.

4.3.2 Job Satisfaction

We examine research subquestion 6b: *Is offering demand-driven pre-screened job training related to higher job satisfaction?* This information is based on our telephone surveys. However, note that we had

Table 4.7
Cox Regressions of the Effect of Treatment on Job Duration (Hazard Rate Odds-Ratios)

	Odds Ratio
ITT	1.092
	(0.895)
TOT	1.086
	(0.902)
# Obs.	647
# Study IDs	294

NOTES: This analysis is considered confirmatory. Each cell is from a separate regression. *P*-values are reported in parentheses and clustered, with clusters defined at the training-cohort level for treated individuals and at the individual (across time) level for control individuals. Each regression additionally controls for baseline randomization strata characteristic (gender, binary age, baseline employment status, and binary baseline income), cohort, and an indicator for holding the job in the quarter prior to the end of training. The Cox regression additionally controls for right-censoring for job duration spans ending at the end of our data span. Inference is adjusted using Benjamini and Hochberg's (1995) procedure, with all coefficients in the table in one domain.

low response rates—26 percent for the treatment group and 9 percent for the control group. The nonresponse weights are therefore especially important for these results; the weighting is described in Appendix B.3. Even with these weights, these results should be interpreted with caution due to the overall low response rates, sizable difference between the response rates of the treatment and control individuals, and—for a subset of the survey respondents—uncertain treatment status (see Appendix B.3). For this reason, we classify this analysis as exploratory instead of as confirmatory and again suggest caution in interpretation of these findings.

It is important to consider nonpecuniary benefits of a job to fully understand the success of labor market interventions (Baird, 2017). In the survey, we ask employed individuals the question, "Are you currently satisfied with your main work or job?" The results are shown in Table 4.8. The job satisfaction variable ranges from 0 (strongly disagree) to 3 (strongly agree). For simplicity of the analysis, we estimate this assuming the Likert scale is a cardinal measure of satisfaction. Details are contained in Appendix B.

We find that treatment assignment or receipt led to higher job satisfaction. When we split the sample by the timing of the survey, while not significant, the TOT analysis shows that the treatment effects were larger in the follow-up period than the interview soon after the end of training, as we would expect given the time it would take to find an improved job. The treatment effect is also relatively large; noting from Table B.2 that the standard deviation of job satisfaction for the control

Table 4.8
Regressions of the Effect of Treatment on Job Satisfaction

	All Periods	Post-Training Baseline	Follow-Up
ITT, satisfied (0–3)	0.386*	0.427	0.364
	(0.079)	(0.233)	(0.347)
TOT, satisfied (0–3)	0.466*	0.458	0.492
	(0.066)	(0.286)	(0.256)
# Obs. (ITT, LATE)	109, 96	72, 62	37, 34
# Persons (ITT, LATE)	86, 76	72, 62	37, 34

NOTE: LATE = local average treatment effect. This analysis is considered exploratory. Each cell is from a separate regression. Regressions additionally control for the p-values, calculated using 2,499 wild bootstrap replications (null imposed). Bootstrap clusters are defined at the training-cohort level for treated individuals and at the individual (across time) level for control individuals. Replication Wald tests are robust to bootstrap clusters and individuals participating in more than one cohort. Each regression additionally controls for baseline randomization strata characteristic (gender, binary age, baseline employment status, and binary baseline income). There are fewer observations for the TOT model, given this requires knowing whether participants attended or not, which requires a clean match between the telephone surveys and our training records. In the desire to include as many individuals as possible from the telephone survey, we include the persons for whom we cannot match names in the training records and thus do not know their attendance status. *** indicates p-values smaller than 0.01; ** indicates p-values smaller than 0.05; * indicates p-values smaller than 0.1.

group is around 1, the TOT results are around one-half a standard deviation increase in job satisfaction, relative to the control group.

We are also able to leverage two additional questions from the survey to relate training experiences to job satisfaction. The first question asked participants if training helped them find a better paid job,[5] while the second asked if training helped them succeed in their current job.[6] Taking one of these variables at a time, we interact each of the four levels of this response with treatment to show how the treatment effects differ depending on whether the training was helpful. The regression still includes both treatment and control groups. As these two questions are only asked of the treatment group but we desire to view differences in the responses by these subgroups, we impute the missing values for the control group and then estimate the model using the observed responses for the treatment group and the imputed responses for the control group. The model and the strong assumptions it relies on are explained in more detail in Appendix B.4.3.

The estimated differences are shown in Figure 4.6. As we might expect, the favorable effects on job satisfaction listed in Table 4.8 seem, in Figure 4.6, to be related to some extent to those who report that training helped them succeed in their current job or with finding a better paid job. In fact, the treatment effects are negative for those who report that the training did not help in those regards. However, these results should be interpreted with caution, especially because we are now taking the already small sample and looking at effects within subgroups of the sample and because we imputed the missing responses of the independent variable of interest for the control group.

4.3.3. Arrests

We examine research subquestion 6c: *Does offering demand-driven pre-screened job training lead to fewer arrests?* Here, we examine the results

---

[5] The question was worded as follows: "On a scale from 1 to 4, how much do you agree with each statement, with 1 being you strongly disagree and 4 being you strongly agree. The training has helped you find a better paid job?"

[6] The question was worded as follows: "On a scale from 1 to 4, how much do you agree with each statement, with 1 being you strongly disagree and 4 being you strongly agree. The training has helped you succeed in your current job?"

**Figure 4.6
ITT Job Satisfaction Regressions by Treatment Status and Reports of
Usefulness of Training in Jobs**

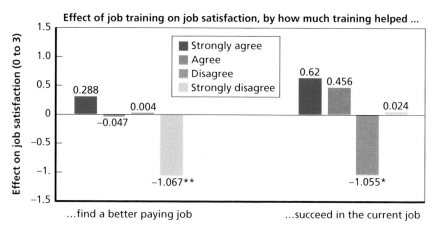

NOTES: This analysis is considered exploratory. Each group of bars is from a separate regression. Regressions additionally control for the four randomization strata and period of survey. Control group training satisfaction values were imputed using multinomial logit model. There were 104 and 105 observations from 84 and 85 unique respondents for the left and right panel, respectively. P-values are calculated using 2,499 wild bootstrap replications (null imposed). Bootstrap clusters are defined at the training-cohort level for treated individuals and at the individual (across time) level for control individuals. Replication Wald tests are robust to bootstrap clusters and individuals participating in more than one cohort. Each regression additionally controls for baseline randomization strata characteristic (gender, binary age, baseline employment status, and binary baseline income). *** indicates p-values smaller than 0.01; ** indicates p-values smaller than 0.05; * indicates p-values smaller than 0.1.

from the regressions of getting arrested after the start of training on treatment status, an indicator for having been arrested prior to the start of training (going back several decades), and the common set of cohort and randomization strata fixed effects. Table 4.9 presents the regression results. The magnitudes of these estimates suggest overall decreases in arrest rates, but none of the estimates were statistically significant. Figure 4.7 presents the results for subgroups. While none of the results are statistically significant, the largest estimated decrease is for men, which represents a decrease of around 9 percentage points (12 percentage points for TOT). Given that the control group's arrest rate is

Table 4.9
Primary Arrest Regressions

	ITT			TOT		
	All	2016 Cohorts	2017 and Later Cohorts	All	2016 Cohorts	2017 and Later Cohorts
	−0.023	−0.292	−0.029	−0.029	−0.361	−0.038
	(0.259)	(0.699)	(0.202)	(0.244)	(0.679)	(0.203)
# Obs.	525	66	459	518	66	452
# Study IDs	464	66	407	458	66	401

NOTES: This analysis is considered confirmatory. Each row is a separate regression, with treatment status, prearrests indicator, and time interacted with the row category. Benjamini and Hechberg (1995) correction is done by cohort grouping (e.g., 2016 cohorts). Wild bootstrap clustered p-values are shown in parentheses. They are calculated using 2,499 wild bootstrap replications (null imposed). Bootstrap clusters are defined at the training-cohort level for treatment, and at the individual (across time) level for control individuals. All regressions control possible time for arrests (from start of treatment until end of data), possible time interacted with treatment status, an indicator for being arrested even before training, for cohort fixed effects, and for strata (gender by employment by income by age) fixed effects. Inference is adjusted using Benjamini and Hochberg's (1995) procedure with domains defined by sample group (e.g., the 2016 cohort analysis using both ITT and TOT are in one domain).

12 percent, this represents a decrease of three-quarters, a substantial impact of the program—though, again, not statistically significant.

4.4. Relationships Between Screening Scores and Outcomes

In this section, we evaluate research question 7: *Do higher prescreening scores relate to improvement in the training completion rate and job placement rates, wages, and employment duration?* Here, we investigate the extent to which the alternative profiling tools were related to attending and completing training, passing final examinations to obtain credentials, and their effects on post-training employment and earnings outcomes. We first examine the predictive power of several of the profiling tool scores. The profiling tools were designed primarily to improve

Figure 4.7
Arrest Regressions by Group

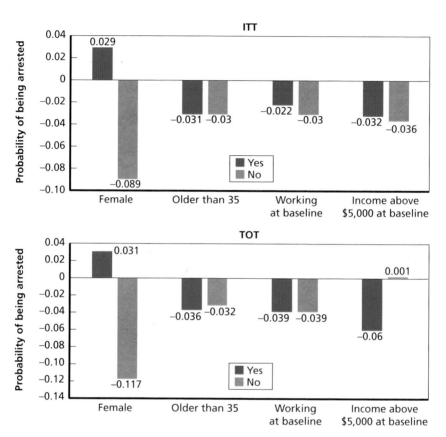

NOTES: This analysis is considered confirmatory. Each grouping of bars is a separate regression, with treatment status, prearrests indicator, and time interacted with the bar's category (e.g., gender). For ITT, there were 459 observations from 407 individuals; for TOT, 452 observations for 401 individuals (multiple Study IDs for some persons caused the difference in numbers). They are calculated using 2,499 wild bootstrap replications (null imposed). Bootstrap clusters are defined at the training-cohort level for treatment, and at the individual (across time) level for control individuals. All regressions control possible time for arrests (from start of treatment until end of data), possible time interacted with treatment status, an indicator for being arrested even before training, for cohort fixed effects, and for strata (gender by employment by income by age) fixed effects. Inference is adjusted using Benjamini and Hochberg's (1995) procedure, with all coefficients in the figure in one domain.

attendance and completion of the training. The first group of variables is constructed from the LWC administrative data set on quarterly earnings and relates to average employment and average earnings before training, as well as prior job stability. The second group of variables is the scores from the different screening tests realized at baseline. These variables are explained in more detail in Table 2.4. In contrast to the variables from the LWC, the results from the screening tests are only available for a smaller number of individuals, in part because not all tests were administered to everyone, and in part because OWD did not retain all scores, and therefore was not able to submit all of them.

For ease of comparison, we converted all variables into standardized scores by demeaning to zero and dividing by the pooled standard deviation of the analytic sample. We use a standardized version (or z-scores) of the scores on the screening tests.

Table 4.10 shows the estimation results. Most coefficients are positive, indicating that individuals with stronger past employment and earnings history, as well as individuals scoring higher on the screening assessments, are more likely to show up for training, complete it, and pass the final examination. However, most of the coefficients are not statistically significant. A notable exception is the TABE score, where we found that scoring one standard deviation higher has a statistically significant effect of over 10 percentage points, on average, on the probability of obtaining a credential, and a positive relationship with all three outcomes, though not statistically significant for attendance or completion. This provides suggestive evidence that, at least with the TABE, the profiling tool was meeting its designed intention of improving program attendance and completion metrics, which was not evident in the other tools (the interview score and the Wonderlic) used for the other cohorts.

Next, we examine how the profiling tools relate to the program effects on employment and earnings outcomes. The model is described in Appendix B. As discussed in Bell and Orr (2002), we are interested in both screening (selecting people with the largest potential treatment effects) and creaming (likelihood of including people who would have seen larger earnings growth whether or not they were trained). Given our RCT design, the coefficient on the profiling tool score represents

Table 4.10
Profiling Tools' Z-Scores Predictions of Training Attendance, Training Completion, and Credential Attainment

	Attended	Completed	Credential	# Obs.	# Study IDs
Average pre-employment	0.043	0.017	0.011	189	189
	(0.133)	(0.509)	(0.669)		
Average pre-earnings	0.033	0.049	0.031	189	189
	(0.157)	(0.222)	(0.465)		
Maximum job tenure	0.039	0.040	0.037	189	189
	(0.242)	(0.168)	(0.226)		
TABE	0.045	0.068	0.114***	144	144
	(0.124)	(0.197)	(0.008)		
Wonderlic	0.040	-0.015	-0.015	47	47
	(0.691)	(0.847)	(0.846)		
Interview score	-0.016	-0.113	0.000	68	68
	(0.714)	(0.153)	(1.000)		

NOTES: This analysis is considered exploratory. Sample includes only individuals randomized into treatment. Each reported coefficient is estimated in a separate regression. P-values are shown in parentheses. They are calculated using 2,499 wild bootstrap replications (null imposed). Bootstrap clusters are defined at the training-cohort level. All regressions control for cohort fixed effects and for strata (gender, employment, income, age) fixed effects. All profiling tools are measured in z-scores for comparability. *** indicates p-values smaller than 0.01; ** indicates p-values smaller than 0.05; * indicates p-values smaller than 0.1.

how a one standard deviation increase in the profiling tool is related to better outcomes, giving us an estimate of the creaming that would occur if the measure was used to select trainees. The coefficient on the interaction of the profiling tool score and treatment status represents how the treatment effect changes with a one standard deviation increase in the profiling tool score, and therefore measures the value of the tool for screening for trainees who would benefit the most from the initiative.

A desirable profiling tool would have screening effects and creaming effects with opposite signs. By choosing candidates with low creaming values, the program would be choosing candidates who would not have good outcomes in the absence of the program. By choosing candidates with high screening values, the program would be choosing candidates who would benefit the most from the program.

Table 4.11 shows the estimated values for creaming and screening. For employment, there are small, insignificant, and mostly positive effects for both creaming and screening. Average pre-employment creams the most, which might be expected, given that it is the baseline version of the outcome. The highest screening, though not statistically significant, is for the Wonderlic score. The worst is the interview score. As for the quarterly earnings, the prior employment variables heavily cream the sample, with no subsequent screening, and therefore are poor policy choices for selecting candidates for training. The interview score, though not statistically significant, also does poorly as to the desired goals. The TABE and Wonderlic scores actually do the best, though results are not statistically significant. Nonetheless, further research could investigate the reasons why these two tests fare the best and if these results hold in other training settings.

4.5. Peer Effects

We next investigate research question 8: *Do a trainee's classmates in the training cohort have an effect on the success of the trainee in terms of employment and earnings?* Peers can affect training outcomes in different ways. For instance, the learning environment and participants' motivation can be affected by the class composition. Also, participants could learn both hard and soft skills not only from instructors but also from their peers. The training is also an opportunity to network, which can also help in landing new and better-paying jobs.

To estimate the role of peers and class composition, we used the profiling tool variables constructed from the LWC administrative data set regarding average employment and average earnings before training, prior job stability, and the other tools investigated above. For each person, we constructed their cohort's average, leaving out the individ-

Table 4.11
ITT Effect on Employment and Earnings by Values of the Profiling Tools (OLS Estimates)

Profiling Tool	Outcome: Employment		Outcome: Quarterly Earnings		# Obs.	# Study IDs
	Coefficient for Creaming	Coefficient for Screening	Coefficient for Creaming	Coefficient for Screening		
Average pre-employment	0.065*	0.039	730.279***	20.665	1,215	336
	(0.074)	(0.431)	(0.004)	(0.958)		
Average pre-earnings	0.061	-0.012	1471.539***	-346.200	1,215	336
	(0.209)	(0.863)	(0.002)	(0.573)		
Maximum job tenure	0.064*	0.013	692.709**	70.672	1,215	336
	(0.078)	(0.788)	(0.015)	(0.872)		
TABE score	-0.075	0.120	-351.501	414.608	763	229
	(0.338)	(0.121)	(0.468)	(0.395)		
Wonderlic score	0.094	0.082	143.773	939.851	390	83
	(0.122)	(0.387)	(0.767)	(0.106)		
Interview score	0.033	-0.049	1090.794	-1837.378	178	96
	(0.818)	(0.759)	(0.373)	(0.259)		

NOTES: This analysis is considered exploratory. Each row of effects is estimated in a separate regression. *P*-values are shown in parentheses. They are calculated using 2,499 wild bootstrap replications (null imposed). Bootstrap clusters are defined at the training-cohort level for treated individuals and at the individual (across time) level for control individuals. Replication Wald tests are robust to bootstrap clusters and individuals participating in more than one cohort. All regressions control for cohort fixed effects and for cross-strata (gender, employment, income, age) fixed effects. *** indicates *p*-values smaller than 0.01; ** indicates *p*-values smaller than 0.05; * indicates *p*-values smaller than 0.1.

ual's value of the variable of interest. We constructed two peer measures: the average across individuals randomized into treatment, and the average across individuals who attended treatment. The goal is, as before, to estimate the ITT (using the first peer measure) and the TOT for those who attended training (using the first peer measure to instrument for the second peer measure). When estimating the peer effects for those who attend training, the decision to take up the treatment is endogenous and can be motivated by peers, in part, which is why we need to use the instrumental variables analysis. Figure 4.8 shows the estimation results. Each effect is estimated in a separate regression, as described in Section B.4.5 in the Appendix.[7]

Our previous analysis shows that the training resulted in positive but not statistically significant effects on employment. Interestingly, however, Figure 4.8 shows that the training participants may benefit from exposure to peers with higher rates of employment and job stability in the past. For instance, increasing the average probability of employment pre-training among peers by one standard deviation is associated with an increase of 16 percentage points in the probability that a participant is employed after training. Increases of about one standard deviation in peers' measures of job stability is associated with an increase in the probability of employment post-training (20 percentage points). Furthermore, while we found the interview score not predictive of screening, we did find that a trainee's peer's interview score is very much related to outcomes.

Therefore, the picture emerging from Figure 4.8 is that participants benefit from peers with better employment histories. We cannot assess whether these gains are coming from better learning through class interactions, increased motivation, networking effects, or other mechanisms. This is an interesting research avenue for future evaluations of similarly randomized training programs.

---

[7]   As an additional check, we performed a separate analysis for the individuals randomized to the control condition. Reassuringly, none of the peers-effects for the controls were statistically significantly different from zero, as we would expect since they did not form a group. This is also notable for being a test of selection into cohorts; that there is no effect reassures us that our findings for the treatment group are due to peer influences and not to selection into different quality cohorts.

Figure 4.8
Effect of Average Peers' Screening Variable on Employment and Earnings Among Those Assigned Training

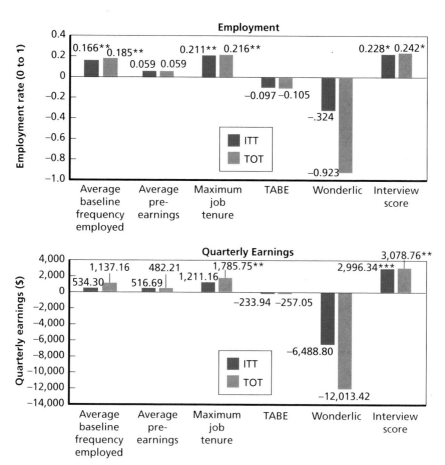

NOTES: This analysis is considered exploratory. Each effect is estimated in a separate regression. Peers are defined based on treatment assignment. *P*-values are shown in parentheses. They are calculated using 2,499 wild bootstrap replications (null imposed). Bootstrap clusters are defined at the training-cohort level for treated individuals and at the individual (across time) level for control individuals. Replication Wald tests are robust to bootstrap clusters and individuals participating in more than one cohort. All regressions control for cross-strata (gender, employment, income, age) fixed effects. Each regression also includes, as a covariate, the individual's own value of the screening variable. *** indicates *p*-values smaller than 0.01; ** indicates *p*-values smaller than 0.05; * indicates *p*-values smaller than 0.1.

4.6. Conclusion

In this chapter, we investigated program participation rates as well as the effect of offering the training program and attendance in that program on several outcomes, including employment status, quarterly earnings, industry of employment, job duration, job satisfaction, and arrests. We find that the training program was successful in several of these areas, at least after the initial two cohorts that began in 2016. After this learning period and changes in the implementation of the program, we found significant increases in quarterly earnings for those in training. These effects were most dramatic for the populations of individuals most in need of the program: those at baseline who were not working or those who had annual individual incomes below $5,000. While we found no overall effect of the program on employment, we did find again that those who entered the program without a job did have a large and statistically significant improvement in their likelihood of being employed after training compared with persons in the control group. We found no meaningful impact on arrests or job duration and found improvements in job satisfaction, though these findings should be read with caution because of data limitations on the survey, most notably in terms of a low and imbalanced response rate that, although we corrected for it as best we could, remains not to the same standard as the other analysis.

We further investigated how the profiling tools related to the success of the program, and found that TABE performed best, both in terms of increasing program attendance, completion, and credentialing, and in terms of screening for those with the higher treatment effects of earnings. However, even these findings were statistically weak and typically not significant. The interview score was never significant and was typically in the wrong direction.

We found evidence of peer effects, especially on the likelihood of being employed after training. Individuals in cohorts with better peers in terms of pre-training average employment rates and job durations were more likely to be employed after training.

## CHAPTER FIVE

Cost-Benefit Analysis

In this chapter, we present findings on the effectiveness of the Career Pathways program through a comparison of the costs and benefits to participants, the public, and society overall. Table 5.1, based on Hollenbeck (2012), shows the components we measure in the cost-benefit analysis and the expected effects for the participants and the public. Plus signs for participants capture expected positive monetary benefits for participants in the program while negative signs denote expected costs to participants. While there are anticipated earnings increases for participants, there are also some monetary costs in the form of increased tax liability, reduced welfare benefits, and forgone earnings while enrolled in training. For the public, plus signs denote increases in monetary benefits (such as increased tax revenue from participants and a reduction in welfare benefit payouts). The only expected monetary cost from the public perspective is the cost of executing the program and providing the training subsidies to program participants. The expected costs and benefits for society represent the summation of the participant and public costs and benefits. Many cost elements for society are represented by a zero, as the participant costs are equally offset by the public benefits, and represent transfers between the groups with no net change. Earnings and fringe benefits are shown as positive elements from society's perspective because there is no cost to the public in addition to the positive participant benefit. Forgone earnings and program costs are an overall negative cost to society and therefore are shown with negative signs in the table. Note that the table does not present a comprehensive list of all the effects from the program. For

Table 5.1
Expected Program Costs and Benefits

Benefits/Costs	Participant	Public	Society
Benefits			
Earnings	+	0	+
Fringe benefits	+	0	+
Taxes	−	+	0
Transfers			
UI	−	+	0
TANF	−	+	0
Food stamps	−	+	0
Medicaid	−	+	0
Costs			
Forgone earnings	−	0	−
Program costs	0	−	−

NOTES: TANF = Temporary Assistance for Needy Families; UI = unemployment insurance. + denotes a net gain; − denotes a net cost, 0 represents net-zero difference.

example, as stated in the logic model, the program may decrease arrests (positive for both participants and public), increase the job satisfaction of participants, and reduce job turnover (and thus reduce hiring costs for employers). These are, in general, difficult effects to monetize. We follow Hollenbeck's rule of thumb to be as conservative as possible in cost-benefit analysis, and thus omit nonmonetized benefits but make every effort to include full costs. The methodology for this chapter is detailed in Appendix C.

Benefits for the participants include changes in net earnings and fringe benefits minus taxes, with potential costs borne in changes in transfers (i.e., higher earnings disqualifying participants from such potential transfers as social welfare programs, and the incidence of higher tax payments). Another benefit we discuss is the reduction in crime due to increases in employment and earnings. Note that some changes in benefits for the participants are exactly offset by the changes for the public. This is the case of higher taxes paid and likely a reduction in transfers received by the participants. Costs for participants include forgone earnings during the period of training, while costs for the public are the subsidies for the training program and the costs of administering the training program.

5.1. Program Costs

We first examine research question 9: *What is the cost per individual completing the program?* We address this question by first estimating the total costs associated with the program. The cost per individual completing the training simply divides the total costs presented in this section by the number of participants completing the program. Table 5.2 summarizes the total costs incurred by calendar year through February 2019.[1] As expected, costs were smaller during the initial stages of the program, with the initial investment limited to some government and contractor staff to manage the program in 2015. Costs increased in 2016 and again in 2017.

The following sections provide additional details of the cost activities in Table 5.2. Note that the sum of government salary and fringe costs presented in Table 5.3 and the overhead for government staff presented in Table 5.4 capture the total OWD government cost in Table 5.2.

5.1.1. OWD Government Costs
Since the beginning of the New Orleans WIF program, OWD has had a varying number of staff providing various levels of support. Table 5.3 summarizes the various OWD job titles and the associated salary and fringe benefits paid out to the staff for each job title. Costs include all

---

[1]   While the program costs are through February 2019, the WIF program participant data is through September 2018, to align with the data used in the outcomes analysis and not include the costs of training these later cohorts, which are also not included in calculations of the benefit.

Table 5.2
Summary of WIF Program Costs

Cost Activity	2015[a]	2016	2017	2018 and 2019[b]	Total Cost	Total Cost per Participant
OWD government	$130,758	$242,109	$326,574	$150,202	$849,641	$2,900
OWD contractor	$30,990	$109,967	$153,305	$161,991	$456,253	$1,557
Participant support payments	$0	$5,730	$592,820	$295,729	$894,279	3,052
Total Cost		$161,747	$357,805	$1,072,699	$607,922	$2,200,173	$7,509

NOTE: Dollar figures adjusted for inflation to 2018.
[a] 2015 is a partial year and includes only OWD government costs beginning in April 2015.
[b] 2018 and 2019 costs are through February 2019; however, the participant costs are through September 2018 to align with the outcome data.

direct costs, including salary and such fringe benefits as government-paid medical insurance, life insurance, workers' compensation insurance, retirement contributions, and other benefits.

In addition to the salary and fringe benefits paid to the government staff, there are overhead charges paid out as well. Table 5.4 summarizes the overhead costs by category.[2]

The following paragraphs describe some of the overhead activities outlined in Table 5.4 in more detail.

5.1.1.1. Outreach Activities

The initial plan for outreach activities was to utilize cultural partners in the New Orleans area to participate in outreach and recruitment activities. As such, memoranda of understanding (MOUs) were established in 2016 between two cultural partners and a fiscal agent acting on behalf of OWD to carry out outreach and recruitment activities. The fiscal agent received $14,900 in WIF funds to manage the cultural partner activities and award payment according to a step function

---

[2]   It should be noted that while OWD incurs costs for the evaluation of the WIF program, those costs are not included in this table. Evaluation costs are considered out of scope for the cost-benefit analysis.

Table 5.3
Salary and Fringe Costs for OWD Government Staff

Job Title	2015[a]	2016	2017	2018 and 2019[b]	Total Cost	Total Cost per Participant
Project manager	$69,246	$95,395	$93,481	$0	$258,122	$881
Infrastructure project lead	$21,818	$81,616	$63,637	$0	$167,072	$570
Deputy director	$14,180	$7,307	$7,468	$19,394	$48,349	$165
Fiscal manager	$11,261	$5,392	$6,529	$18,581	$41,763	$143
Director	$0	$0	$0	$23,603	23,603	$81
Total direct labor and fringe cost	$116,505	$189,710	$171,116	$61,578	$538,909	$1,839

NOTE: Dollar figures adjusted for inflation to 2018.
[a] 2015 is a partial year and includes only OWD government costs beginning in April 2015.
[b] 2018 and 2019 costs are through February 2019.

Table 5.4
Overhead Costs for OWD Government Staff

Overhead Category	2015[a]	2016	2017	2018 & 2019[b]	Total Cost	Total Cost per Participant
Travel	$5,276	$3,658	$0	$0	$8,934	$30
Material and supplies	$3,615	$340	$7,066	–$103	$10,918	$37
Telephone/cell phones	$796	$450	$283	–$24	$1,504	$5
Outreach	$0	$34,865	$43,115	$5,300	$83,281	$284
Curriculum design	$0	$0	$24,150	$0	$24,150	$82
Info sessions	$4,566	$4,137	$3,103	$11,800	$23,606	$81
Rent	$0	$8,948	$22,202	$25,712	$56,862	$194
Data tracking	$0	$0	$55,539	$2,750	$58,289	$199
Indirect	$0	$0	$0	$43,189	$43,189	$147
Total overhead cost	$14,253	$52,398	$155,458	$88,624	$310,732	$1,061

NOTE: Dollar figures adjusted for inflation to 2018.
[a] 2015 is a partial year and includes only OWD government costs beginning in April 2015.
[b] 2018 and 2019 costs are through February 2019.

based on the follow-up and retention of candidates for the WIF program. However, this approach failed to attract many candidates into the program, and any payouts to cultural partners were negligible. The recruitment methods have since been adjusted such that these costs will not recur.

In 2017, OWD entered into a contract with a communications firm to create and deliver outreach material to assist in recruitment. Activities include the development of a WIF video and program logo design and branding. The costs for all outreach activities are captured in Table 5.4.

5.1.1.2. Data Tracking

OWD made investments, with expenditures beginning in 2017, in a workforce development data-tracking tool. This data management system is used to support the implementation of the WIF program. The system tracks data for program participants in the control and treatment group—including demographics, enrollments, assessments, referrals, attendance, services, income, case notes, indicators, and outcomes—specifically for the purposes of measuring impact and improving program performance. Table 5.4 includes the WIF funds invested by OWD to assist in the development of a data management tool. This includes the procurement of ten Microsoft Dynamics customer relationship management software licenses and a software development firm to tailor the product to OSD needs.

5.1.1.3. Curriculum Design

OWD partnered with several organizations, including nonprofits and other local governments, to participate in the National Green Infrastructure Certification Program ("National Green Infrastructure Certification Program," 2019). The aim of this program is to develop and implement a certification program to establish a protocol for the certification of individuals to perform specific green infrastructure work. The city of New Orleans' desire to develop green expertise in its local labor force led to its investment in the certification program. Table 5.4 includes the WIF funds invested by OWD in the development of this certification program.

It should be noted that we interviewed the training partners to gather potential costs incurred by the training partners in support of the WIF program. However, there were no instances noted where training partners modified the curriculum for the WIF program in ways that required OWD to make payments. All courses, whether in a classroom or online, are the same courses already developed and available to the general public.

5.1.2. OWD Contractor Costs

In addition to government staff, OWD employs contracted support to provide outreach, interview screening, and advising to participants in the program. Like the government staff, the contractor support has had a numerous number of staff providing different levels of support. Table 5.5 summarizes the various OWD job titles and the associated salary and fringe benefits paid out to the staff for each job title. Costs include all direct costs including salary (i.e., take-home pay) and fringe benefits, such as company-paid medical insurance, life insurance, workers' compensation insurance, retirement contributions, and other benefits. The job titles for contract staff help to distinguish among the various activities being conducted. Specifically, some staff are outreach specialists while others specialize in advising.

In addition to the direct labor and fringe benefits paid to contractor staff, there are contractor overhead charges, as well. Table 5.6 summarizes the overhead costs by category.

5.1.3. Participant Support Payment Costs

WIF program participant costs include payouts to an individual training account for each participant and support services costs. These costs are summarized in Table 5.7.

5.2 Program Benefits

We next evaluate research question 10: *What is the value of the benefits of the program to the trainee, the government, and to society?* The benefits enumerated for this come from Chapter 4—specifically, from

Table 5.5
Salary and Fringe Costs for OWD Contractor Staff

Job Title	2015[a]	2016	2017	2018 and 2019[b]	Total Cost	Cost per Participant
WIF business consultant	$9,048	$24,517	$24,941	$9,475	$67,981	$232
Project director	$2,556	$8,106	$5,467	$0	$16,129	$55
WIF outreach specialist	$0	$13,787	$35,844	$48,659	$98,290	$335
Project accountant	$0	$0	$203	$198	$401	$1
Quality assurance analyst	$0	$0	$0	$5,466	$5,466	$19
Receptionist	$0	$1,501	$2,389	$899	$4,788	$16
WIF career advisor	$9,105	$29,791	$41,753	$48,840	$129,488	$442
Total salary costs	$20,709	$77,702	$110,596	$113,537	$322,544	$1,101
Total fringe benefits costs	$2,502	$10,999	$18,316	$21,010	$52,827	$180
Total salary and fringe cost	$23,211	$88,700	$128,912	$134,547	$375,370	$1,281

NOTE: Dollar figures adjusted for inflation to 2018.
[a] 2015 is a partial year and includes only OWD costs beginning in April 2015.
[b] 2018 and 2019 costs are through February 2019.

Table 5.6
Overhead Costs for OWD Contractor Staff

Job Title	2015[a]	2016	2017	2018 and 2019[b]	Total Cost	Cost Per Participant
Postage	$0	$0	$0	$12	$12	$0
Travel	$0	$939	$920	$0	$1,859	$6
Material and supplies	$1,034	$2,177	$1,557	$568	$5,337	$18
Equipment purchases	$1,101	$1,669	$569	$0	$3,339	$11
Phones	$140	$414	$270	$0	$825	$3
Recruiting drug testing	$79	$138	$59	$0	$276	$1
Insurance	$401	$397	$0	$0	$799	$3
Accounting and audit	$0	$8	$7	$0	$15	$0
Miscellaneous	$966	$1,150	$347	$364	$2,828	$10
Indirect	$2,581	$9,138	$13,364	$15,464	$40,546	$138
Management fee	$1,476	$5,237	$7,300	$11,037	$25,049	$85
Total overhead cost	$7,778	$21,267	$24,393	$27,444	$80,882	$276

NOTE: Dollar figures adjusted for inflation to 2018.
[a] 2015 is a partial year and includes only OWD costs beginning in April 2015.
[b] 2018 and 2019 costs are through February 2019.

Table 5.7
WIF Program Participant Costs

Cost Category	2016	2017	2018[a]	Total Cost	Total Cost per Participant
Individual training account payout	$1,230	$533,498	$250,773	$785,501	$2,681
Support services payout	$4,499	$59,322	$44,956	$108,778	$371
Total participant cost	$5,730	$592,820	$295,729	$894,279	$3,052

NOTE: Dollar figures adjusted for inflation to 2018.
[a] 2018 costs are through September 2018

Table 4.4 and the earnings return to the program. This is scaled to account for fringe benefits accompanying jobs, as described in Appendix C. As explained, we are conservative in considering only this benefit, discounting our findings of potential effects on job satisfaction and arrests reduction (though these results were either deemed exploratory or were not statistically significant). The effect of the increased earnings also leads to higher taxes and lower government program transfers (both net zero at the society level, as it represents a gain for public perfectly offset by a loss to the participants). We also allow for forgone earnings in the form of lower earnings during the training period.

5.3. Cost-Benefit Results

Using the findings from Sections 5.1 on costs and 5.2 on benefits, we are able to address research question 11: *What are the resulting cost-benefit net values of the program, including the IRRs and ROIs, and how many years does it take for benefits to exceed costs?*

Table 5.8 summarizes the benefits and costs associated with the WIF program from the perspective of the participant, the public, and society, based on the calculations and methods discussed above. It considers a short-run time frame of three years and longer-term time frame of 30 years. In a similar fashion to Hollenbeck (2012), we felt it appropriate to compare a relatively short period of three years in which soci-

Table 5.8
Participant, Public, and Society Benefits and Costs Per Participant

Benefit/Cost	3 Years				30 Years			
	Participant (2016 Cohorts)	Participant (2017 and Later Cohorts)	Public	Society[a]	Participant (2016 Cohorts)	Participant (2017 and Later Cohorts)	Public	Society[a]
Benefits								
Earnings	-$13,140	$8,899	$0	$7,015	-$13,140	$49,785	$0	$47,901
Fringe benefits	-$5,061	$3,427	$0	$2,702	-$5,061	$19,175	$0	$18,449
Taxes	$2,323	-$1,573	$1,240	$0	$2,323	-$8,800	$8,467	$0
Transfers								
UI	$0	-$825	$825	$0	$0	-$4,613	$4,613	$0
TANF	$0	-$861	$861	$0	$0	-$1,368	$1,368	$0
SNAP	$0	-$969	$969	$0	$0	-$5,423	$5,423	$0
Medicaid	$0	-$735	$735	$0	$0	-$4,114	$4,114	$0
Costs								
Forgone earnings	-$903	-$78	$0	-$208	-$904	-$79	$0	-$208
WIF program costs	$0	$0	-$7,509	-$7,509	$0	$0	-$7,509	-$7,509
Net Benefits/Costs	-$16,781	$7,285	-$2,879	$2,001	-$16,781	$44,564	$16,476	$58,634[b]
IRR (quarterly real rate)	N/A	N/A	-6.46%	10.74%	N/A	N/A	5.72%	15.93%
ROI (annualized rate)	-360.01%	355.28%	-14.88%	7.99%	-210.03%	23.57%	3.95%	7.44%

NOTE: N/A = not applicable. Dollar figures adjusted for inflation to 2018.
[a] Note that, as mentioned in the body of the report, the society column for both the three- and 30-year estimates are not a simple summation of the participant and public columns. Again, this is due to the fact that the 2016 participant data are treated as a fixed learning-curve cost which is then distributed to later cohorts. For example, in the case of earnings, the *total* negative earning estimate for 2016 cohort participants is divided by the number of participants in cohorts after 2016 and therefore reduces the assumed earnings from the perspective of society. This same approach holds true for the other cost elements.
[b] The table shows the results assuming a 5-percent discount rate. The 30-year net benefits and costs to society, assuming a discount rate range of 3 to 10 percent, result in a net benefit and cost range of $32,022–$77,440.

ety might begin to see positive net benefits with a longer period of 30 years to capture when earnings for current participants might begin to end as they near retirement age. As shown in Table 5.9, we also looked at the cumulative net benefits through the first five years to capture how the net benefits change over time. Appendix C describes in detail the assumptions and methodologies used to extrapolate costs and benefits to 30 years from only several quarters of reported data. For participants, the benefits and costs are separated into the two 2016 cohorts and all of the remaining cohorts in 2017 and later. This reflects our findings that the program had an upfront learning curve with no returns to the program for the first two cohorts, and the cohorts that followed have, on average, positive earnings. This distinction is evident in Table 5.8, in which we compare the benefits and costs of participants early in the program with those later in the program. It is important to include these early cohorts in the analysis because they demonstrate early challenges in program implementation, and these are potential costs to any program as the implementers learn and adapt during early

Table 5.9
Cumulative Net Benefits and Costs by Year, and Break-Even Year

	Participant (2016 Cohorts)	Participant (2017 and Later Cohorts)	Public	Society
By Year 1	−$9,694	$2,499	−$5,956	−$4,847
By Year 2	−$14,877	$4,952	−$4,412	−$1,593
By Year 3	−$16,781	$7,285	−$2,879	$2,001
By Year 4	−$16,781	$9,505	−$1,382	$5,718
By Year 5	−$16,781	$11,618	$42	$9,255
Break-even year	Never	Year 1	Year 5	Year 3

implementation. These early challenges and negative results are real economic costs that should be captured in any cost-benefit analysis.[3]

In order to account for the public and societal costs of the program, given this separated cohorts approach, we assume that the 2016 cohorts are a fixed learning curve investment, while the 2017 and later cohorts can be scaled to more trainees thereafter. In essence, to sum up to the public and society levels, we multiply the benefits and costs of the 2016 cohorts by the total number of persons assigned to training in these cohorts (42, including veterans), and then divide this product by the trainees in the later cohorts (293, including veterans), with the concept being that the costs of the initial cohorts are distributed across however many trainees that follow. For example, the first benefits row in Table 5.8 captures the estimated earnings impact per participant randomly assigned to the treatment group as discussed in the methodology and data section above. Over three years, the estimated losses for the 2016 cohorts is $13,140, while the gains to 2017 and later cohorts was estimated to be $8,899.[4] The total earnings impact on a per-participant basis from a societal perspective is therefore slightly less than the earnings impact for all cohorts after 2016 alone, as we capture the

---

[3] For the 2017 and later cohorts, despite finding that the earnings gap increased with more time elapsed after the end of the program (see Figure 4.3), we assume a more conservative constant difference in earnings thereafter at the sample average ITT estimate from Table 4.7. For the 2016 cohorts, we followed a different strategy in which we allowed the earnings losses implied by Table 4.7 to decrease to zero with time and stay at zero thereafter. We did this for two reasons: first, in results not presented in this report, the analogous analysis of Figure 4.3 for the 2016 cohorts shows a negative ITT estimate that converges toward zero instead of diverging away from zero as in the 2017 and later cohorts. Second, unlike the 2017 cohorts, the ITT estimate of Table 4.7 for quarterly earnings for the 2016 cohorts is not statistically significant. Given the small sample, we fit a model that allowed for a linear time trend for the ITT and used the estimated ITT for each quarter it was negative until it reached zero; thereafter, it was left at zero. This happens in the fourth year after the end of training.

[4] In the longer-term (30 years) columns, it should be noted that the 2016 cohort losses are the same as the shorter-term (three years) columns, at an estimated $13,140. This is because the analysis, as discussed in Chapter 4, showed that the losses of these cohorts gradually diminished over time and, by year four, the losses turned positive. The results were not statistically significant, however; as a conservative assumption, we assumed that by year four, there would be no assumed lost or gained earnings in our cost-benefit model.

cost of early program losses to earnings. The same is true for fringe benefits and taxes. As shown, tax revenue is a benefit to the public, though, as expected, the tax revenue benefit to the public is less than it would otherwise be if we did not include the 2016 cohorts: The impact to tax revenue is actually an estimated $2,323 loss to the public for the 2016 cohorts because of their lost earnings. If we were to exclude the lost tax revenue from the 2016 cohorts, the public tax benefit would be equal to the 2017 and later participant loss in tax payouts. The societal tax impact is zero, however, as it must be true that the net participant payouts (or nonpayouts in the case of 2016 cohorts) must be equal to the public revenue from tax receipts (or nonreceipts in the case of 2016 cohorts). This logic for earnings, fringe benefits, and taxes applies in both the three-year and 30-year sets of columns.

For transfers, the 2016 cohorts saw no net changes in welfare benefits such as UI, TANF, the Supplemental Nutrition Assistance Program (SNAP), and Medicaid. That is, there were no reductions in those receiving these benefits in the first two cohorts. The method for estimating these impacts for all participants is included in the methodology and data section in previous sections of this chapter. As expected, the loss in these benefits is equally offset by the fact that the public no longer needs to pay these benefits. The net impact to society is therefore zero. For example, as shown in Table 5.8, we estimate the net impact to UI benefits as a loss of $825 per participant and a gain to the public of $825 over three years, and a loss of $4,613 per participant and a gain to the public of $4,613 over 30 years. The net impact to society is therefore $0.

Program costs are simply the total costs of the program on a per-participant basis using all program participants from the 2016 cohorts and later. This is captured by the public and societal cost of $7,509 on the WIF program cost row in Table 5.8. The program costs are all public costs, because the costs to start and operate the program and the participant subsidies are all publicly funded. Forgone earnings are based on OLS estimates and the societal impact of forgone earnings includes both the relatively large negative impact to the 2016 cohorts as well as the much smaller impact to 2017 and later cohorts. The 2016 cohort impact is a $903 loss per participant, while the 2017 and later cohort impact is a much smaller $78 loss per participant. The relatively small forgone earnings impact is partly due to a fairly short training period[5] and the fact that many trainees continued to work, and it is based on the estimates comparing the adjusted average treatment and control group earnings through OLS regressions during the quarters in which individuals were being trained.[6] It should also be noted that the costs are the same in the three-year time frame and 30-year time frame. This is because forgone earnings only capture those earnings forgone during training participation and the program costs only capture those costs to provide the initial subsidy for training and costs to manage the WIF program during the initial time frame of the program. A discussion of the methodology and data used to calculate the benefits and costs in Table 5.8 are summarized in the previous section. All future benefits are discounted to 2018 dollars assuming a 5-percent discount rate. There are several conceptual bases for determining the appropriate discount rate, including potential returns on private savings options (e.g., the interest rate on treasury bills) or the potential return to entrepreneurs' investments in the private sector. While there is no consensus in the literature on the proper discount rate to use in such analyses, according to Levin and McEwan (2000), rates between 0 percent and 11 percent are often used. As such, 5 percent seems to be a reasonable rate to use as a baseline assumption. We also show the impact to 30-year net benefits and costs with a 3-percent and 10-percent discount rate in the footnote to Table 5.8, to demonstrate how sensitive the results are to the discount rate. All costs are adjusted for inflation to 2018 dollars. Costs for forgone wages are also discounted with the same 5-percent rate because they extend slightly beyond one quarter. Program costs are not discounted because there are no future costs included in the analysis.

---

[5] The training time was two to four months.

[6] Specifically, we estimated the primary model of the impact of the program on earnings (Table 4.5) as presented in Appendix B.2, equation B.3, but instead of including post-training quarters of earnings, we included only the quarters that occurred during training for the treatment group, and for the control group, the same quarters as their comparison treatment group was in training.

Table 5.8 also shows the net benefits and costs, IRR, and ROI for the average participant from the perspective of the 2016 cohort participants, the 2017 and later cohort participants, the public, and society. These metrics are also shown for both a three- and 30-year time frame.

The IRR is a calculation that determines the discount rate required to make the net present value of future cash flows equal to zero. Put another way, it is the rate required to equalize the benefits and costs in present-value terms. This calculation is not included for participants, but for different reasons in the cases of the 2016 and 2017 and later cohorts. For the 2016 cohorts, the IRR is not calculated because the costs in lost earnings through year three are never made up as the model assumes earnings impacts are zero beginning in year four and continue on at zero into the future. For the 2017 and later cohorts, the IRR is not calculated because the only costs to participants (forgone earnings during training period) are immediately overwhelmed by the earnings within a quarter. There is essentially no time required to pay for the participants' small investment in forgone earnings.

The annualized ROI is calculated by the following equation:

$$ROI = \left(\frac{Benefits}{Costs} \right)^{1\text{-}t} - 1$$

where t equals the number of years. Unsurprisingly, the ROI from the participants' perspective is extremely large in the negative direction for the 2016 cohorts, and extremely large in the positive direction for the 2017 and later cohorts, particularly in the short run. As noted in the IRR calculation from the perspective of participants, the benefits are very large relative to the costs. This is also evident in the 355.28-percent ROI for the WIF program from the participant perspective. Over the long run, this ROI shrinks with the assumption that the earnings gap remains constant between the treatment and control groups and earnings in the distant future are highly discounted in present-value terms.

Turning to the public perspective, the benefits do not overcome the costs in the first three years as demonstrated by a negative IRR and ROI. The public benefits of increased tax revenue and lower payouts for welfare benefits are not enough to overcome the fairly substantial subsidy and program costs in the first three years. Over the long term, the benefits eventually become large enough to justify the costs strictly from the public perspective. According to the results, the benefits would begin to overcome the costs in five years. The year in which each category breaks even (e.g., the year in which benefits begin to equal costs) is captured in Table 5.9.

Finally, from a societal perspective, combining the participant and public benefits and costs, the ROIs are positive in the short run. The return is fairly substantial in both the short and long runs.

Table 5.9 shows that in only three years, from a cost-benefit perspective, society benefits from this program. In the first five rows of Table 5.9, the cumulative net benefits (i.e., benefits minus costs) are shown at the end of each given year. The last column points out the break-even year for each societal group. As expected, the Year 3 row net benefits in Table 5.9 are the same as the net benefits in the "3 Years" time frame shown in the first four columns of Table 5.8. Table 5.9 shows at what point the benefits begin to outweigh the costs of the program. As already discussed, the costs to 2016 cohorts are never overcome by benefits in our cost-benefit model. However, for 2017 and later cohorts, the benefits immediately outweigh the costs to participants because the training stipend is completely a public cost. At year five, the public begins to realize a positive net benefit. For society as a whole, including all participants and the public, net benefits are positive by year three.

5.4. Conclusion

Consistent with the positive findings earlier in the report, the cost-benefit findings show encouraging results. Both the participants and the public benefit from the implementation of the job training program with immediate benefits to participants, particularly after a program implementation learning period. The participant benefits include increased earnings and associated fringe benefits. While the public benefits are slower to accrue relative to the program costs and training stipends, increased tax revenue and decreased welfare payouts offset these costs in a relatively short time frame by the end of year five. As a result of the significant benefit to participants and eventual positive benefit to the public, it is not surprising that society as a whole has benefited from this program in a relatively short time frame. Despite early investment costs and participant losses in the form of decreased earnings for some of the first cohorts, the significant gains from later cohorts enabled this initiative to see positive returns fairly quickly.

## CHAPTER SIX

Discussion of Findings

Our study of this job training intervention generated several valuable findings. Overall, we found that the intervention as originally envisioned was problematic but that the city was agile in its adaptation, utilizing lessons learned, and this ultimately proved relatively successful with positive, meaningful increases in earnings associated with the program, as well as increases in job satisfaction, though these results should be interpreted with caution. There were not significant changes to employment rates, job duration, or arrests. Our research adds to the three strains of literature discussed earlier by showing an example of an effective WIA program, reinforcing the importance of demand-driven job training programs, and showing that the screening and creaming questions are difficult to assess for many reasons. In this chapter, we discuss all of the findings.

The initial idea to use hospitality and leisure firms and cultural partners to screen did not work. A major change in the Career Pathways program involved the nature of the screening, which had implications for the type of training that was likely to be most successful. As originally proposed, hospitality industry employers would screen their current employees and refer individuals who were judged to have the work habits and aptitude for obtaining more training that would allow them to move to a higher-wage job. It was thought that these employers would be willing to refer their good employees to the program because they realized that these employees were likely to leave anyway due to a lack of opportunity in their current jobs and because the employers could use the promise of the Career Pathway program to recruit eager and capable replacements. However, the combination of various factors, such as political conflicts and reevaluation of the cost of referring incumbent employees, resulted in the hospitality employers deciding not to participate. OWD's attempt to replace this screening and referral pipeline with similar screening by community cultural partners based on long-standing relationships with candidates was also unsuccessful. The resulting replacement of the profiling tool with a more formal—albeit transient—interview and testing process performed by workforce development professionals who had no relationship with the candidates changed the nature of the screening substantially.

It is not clear whether the initial idea of using low-skill, low-wage industries to provide a source of trainees for a cross-industry pipeline could work in other settings, despite its failure in New Orleans with the hospitality and leisure industry. We are inclined to believe that it generally would not be workable, and would require a very specific type of industry and employers, where the goal of the employers is only temporary hiring and afterward the trainee transitions into a different firm or industry. This may be the result, for example, of a mission-driven nonprofit firm that seeks to provide transitions from unemployment to employment. However, these firms are unlikely to be sufficiently large in any given location to account for job training recruitment needs.

It was not clear whether the sole use of cultural partners as sources of potential trainees would ever succeed. The goal here was to use those partners' more-intimate knowledge of their members' soft skills to form reasonable predictions about the likelihood of each candidate completing training and engaging in such a way as to make the training efficacious. From the start, there were concerns that using cultural partners would not be generalizable to cities other than New Orleans, and we learned in this analysis that even in New Orleans, where these organizations exist and plausibly would want their members to receive training and better employment, the organizations were largely unable to provide a sufficient number of potential recruits and seemed to recommend all potential candidates, negating the usefulness of the screening mechanism. Perhaps the use of cultural partners could succeed in cities where such organizations exist in sufficient number, if certain actions were taken. First, the cultural partners would have to be better educated as to the reason for a meaningful screen and given reassurances that those who fail the screening would receive support. Second, the cultural partners would likely need to receive resource support to make the endeavor feasible financially. It is unclear whether these two measures would be sufficient to make such a partnership successful, but they could improve the likelihood of a positive relationship and outcomes.

OWD was reflective during early implementation; there is evidence that this may have improved the implementation and impacts of the program. Creating a pipeline to career pathways is a challenging endeavor. Many of the features of the proposed design were modified as OWD learned what worked and what did not work in the initial plan. Our findings indicate that OWD was reflective during the early implementation stages and continually adjusted strategies in response to the realities of the political and economic environment in which the Career Pathways program is embedded, as well as in response to organizational capacity. OWD attempted to stay faithful to the mission of the Career Pathways program while adjusting its design and strategies as needed. When the hospitality and leisure sector resisted referring employees and otherwise partnering on the Career Pathways program and the cultural partners did not have sufficient capacity to recruit the necessary numbers of candidates nor the incentive to properly screen, OWD opened the pipeline to the public through several recruitment methods and conducted the screening process in-house. Although this resulted in changes in the population targeted, the training still catered to those in need (underemployed and unemployed) even if they were recruited from other sectors or had no previous work history. Similarly, when industry demand for a skilled workforce halted in the energy sector job market, OWD expanded the Career Pathways program to include training in health care and IT, the latter of which is aligned with the Mayor's Office of Economic Development's strategic priorities and with the labor market needs in the greater New Orleans area, according to OWD.

We found that the changes may have been successful. Specifically, treatment effects and thus ROI improved drastically after the first set of training cohorts, after changes had been made. The training program overall required this burn-in period, where adjustments were made, processes were refined, and relationships were strengthened.

At times, the training curriculum was not tailored to the needs of the trainees. Though the educational institutions selected to participate in the program as training providers have extensive expertise in delivering coursework in the program areas of these trainings, there were areas of the program that could have been modified to better address the needs of participants instead of using preexisting coursework. The trainings could have incorporated even more hands-on experiences to improve participant employability and satisfaction. Furthermore, the curricula could have been structured to promote more soft skills or teach competencies that traditionally lead to increased likelihood of employability. For example, the curricula could incorporate opportunities for trainees to work in teams by including group work in the lesson plans. Similarly, the curricula could develop participants' communication skills by requiring them to participate in classwide discussions and presentations. Other skills, such as responsibility and professionalism, could also be developed by having clear class expectations regarding attendance and completing assignments.

The relationship with firms was not sufficiently strong post-training. While the relationships with local firms were sufficient to produce redirection away from the energy industry (given falling oil prices) towards health care and IT, training participants noted a significant lack in facilitation of post-training connections to firms in target industries. There was no evidence of program funds being used for on-the-job training, as was allowed, and treatment group individuals were not statistically more likely to report receiving support in employer connections than the control group was receiving from the WDB. The Career Pathways program could have been stronger and potentially led to even better outcomes if there had been stronger relationships with the firms in the target industries.

The training program was successful in increasing earnings of program participants in later cohorts, but there is no evidence of impact on employment. While the first two cohorts were not successful in producing higher earnings, from 2017 and later, the remaining 13 cohorts in our employment and earnings analysis produced, on average, meaningful earnings increases for those assigned to the treatment group—$804 per quarter for our primary specification, and over $1,000 for those who attended training from the TOT estimates. The overall treatment effect of $804 represents a sizable improvement in earnings. Given the control group's average quarterly earnings per participant in the post-training period was $3,317, treatment assignment caused an approximately 25-percent increase in quarterly earnings. These results compare favorably with the research on job training programs (e.g., Andersson et al., 2013, with quarterly earnings gains for two other WIA-funded programs of between $236 and $2,056; Heinrich et al., 2013, finding gains of around $600 across several WIF-funded training programs; and Maguire et al., 2010, finding earnings gains of 18.3 percent). Meanwhile, we found no impact overall for employment rates, except for individuals who entered training without a job.

There is an important learning curve for implementation of job training. We find negative and statistically significant effects on earnings and employment for the initial two cohorts. Later cohorts were significantly better, which we account to OWD making necessary changes in recruitment and screening, improvements in curriculum and industry partners, and overall growth over time. While we are not able to separate out these competing reasons for the improvements (which happened more or less simultaneously), this suggests that local governments implementing job training programs should be patient and not eliminate a program if it does not succeed in its first or second iterations. If the evaluation ended after looking only at the 2016 cohorts, there would have been strong evidence to eliminate this program, which could have been premature. Meanwhile, we find strong evidence of favorable cost-benefit later on, and even including these initial cohorts. There should be space for the relationships and programs to mature, at least past their first or second attempts, if there is reason to believe in the ultimate success of the program.

The pathways with the best outcomes were those with more-involved industry partners. Outcomes were worst in AM; one of the target industries withdrew at the beginning (energy) and there was further withdrawal of support from local firms in helping develop curriculum. The best outcomes seem to have been with industries that were more involved. For example, in the health care pathway, Oschner was one of the training providers; as one of the most important employers in the region, it gave crucial support for the training process and post-training outcomes (even if no one was assured employment). While we cannot demonstrate a causal relationship between industry involvement and outcomes, these results are suggestive of a possible connection.

There are suggestive nonearning improvements in outcomes from training. We find higher job satisfaction and some evidence for placement in target industries. The job satisfaction results should be read with caution because of low survey response rates. On the other hand, we found no effect for job persistence. This might not be surprising, as there may have been countervailing forces from treatment, leading trainees to be more likely to leave bad jobs (shorter job persistence) while placing them in positions that are more stable, with skills that make them less likely to be let go (longer job persistence). A longer post-training measurement would be necessary to properly investigate and separate these two factors. We also found no real effect for employment status, with training having the real effect of increasing earnings in jobs, and not increasing the likelihood of holding any job in the quarter. We should note that there were large effects on employment status for those who entered training without a job. Finally, we did not find any statistical evidence of an impact on arrests.

The impact of training on earnings is larger for specific subgroups of individuals. We find the largest treatment effects for older persons, those who entered randomization with no job, and the most poor (prior annual incomes below $5,000). This is very encouraging for the purposes of the training program, especially that the earnings increases and employment effects are largest for those most in need prior to training. These results also stand in contrast to some of the prior literature, which found the weakest effects of job training programs for displaced workers without a job (Andersson et al., 2013; Heinrich et al., 2013). Women had higher earnings gains than men, though the difference between the impacts on the two subgroups was not statistically significant.

Trainees have better outcomes if their training cohort peers have better prior employment histories. We find evidence of peer effects. Individuals whose fellow trainees have a better history of being frequently employed are more likely to be placed into jobs at the end of training and more likely to have better earnings. This may be due to a better classroom environment, networking creating better opportunities after training, or other unexamined factors.

There is no evidence that the screening interviews produced the intended effects, although the TABE operated better. The hope was that the screening interviews would lead to lower attrition from training and better post-training outcomes. While we were unable to compare against an unscreened population, we did compare those with higher and lower interview scores, and found that scores were not related to these desired outcomes. If anything, screening interviews serve as a creaming tool, selecting individuals likely to succeed whether or not they participated in training. On the other hand, the TABE, a basic literacy and numeracy test, is related to higher program completion, credentialing, and better treatment effects for higher scores (screening) with lower creaming effects, though these effects generally are not statistically significant. However, it is worth exploring in the literature how the TABE (and potentially a combination of other screening tools) is related to the desired outcomes of training completion and credentialing. It would be better to select those participants who would benefit the most from training (screening) and, where possible, avoid those who would have the best outcomes regardless of whether they were trained (anti-creaming).

Overall, we find the program has high ROI. For participants, the benefits of the program almost immediately exceed the costs (increased earnings exceeding the fractional loss in social benefits, the increased taxes, and the forgone earnings during training). For the public, five years are needed to make up the implementation costs, in terms of decreased welfare transfers and increased tax returns. For society, less than four years are needed for benefits to exceed costs, and there is a societal three-year annualized ROI of 7.99 percent—and 7.44 percent over 30 years. This makes this overall intervention a good investment, especially as this calculation is conservative: It does not account for all of the realized benefits, such as improved job satisfaction and potential decreases in arrests for men.

## CHAPTER SEVEN

Conclusion

In evaluating the Career Pathways job training program for unemployed and underemployed workers in New Orleans, we had many findings to be optimistic about. While there was a slow start to the effectiveness of the program, after the first few cohorts of training, we found meaningful increases in earnings post-training as well as some suggestive evidence of increases in job satisfaction. Most notably, the populations of most interest for this program—unemployed and low-income workers—had large increases in earnings due to training assignment, with those who were unemployed in particular showing substantially larger benefits from the program than those entering the program already employed. While the program deviated from the originally proposed implementation, the adjustments that were made seemed to be related to improvements in effectiveness and to display the agility necessary for success in demand-driven job training. Overall, we find the job training program to be a good return on investment in terms of benefits outweighing costs, both for the individual and for the government—and, ultimately, for society.

While the program was ultimately successful according to several metrics, there are areas in which it could be improved, and there are many takeaways from the study of this program across 25 training cohorts. We have a number of recommendations for future implementations of such job training programs. These recommendations and lessons learned may be of special interest to WIBs and employers who plan to invest in disadvantaged workers, as well as for philanthropic foundations interested in workforce development, researchers interested in this topic, and DOL. Furthermore, these recommendations and lessons could be most applicable to areas similar to New Orleans: urban areas with sizable low-skill, unemployed, and underemployed populations.

Two- to four-month job training programs aimed at low-income individuals can work. Our primary takeaway is that something about this program succeeds in terms of increasing earnings, and there is suggestive evidence of increased job satisfaction. These gains seem to be most prominent among the populations that we most would want to benefit from such a program, namely the lowest-income workers and those not working at the outset of training.

These job training programs are a good return on investment after a burn-in learning curve period: in the very short term for the trainees, in the short term for society, and in the medium term for the government. The positive returns to society suggest that this program demonstrates a good use of public resources and could be a model for future training programs. However, some patience is required—for the government, the benefits of reduced public assistance and increased tax revenues take five years after training to overcome the costs. Looking over a 30-year period, though, the public has a 3.95 percent annualized ROI for these job programs. And these returns are strictly to the government—again, if we include the benefits to the individual so as to calculate societal returns, payoffs come in the third year after training and the 30-year annualized ROI is 7.44 percent, suggesting a very effective program, especially because these calculations are conservative by not including all benefits. While we cannot assure that the same program effectiveness would be realized in other cities and applications of this training model, the gains would be most likely if the circumstances that made the approach successful in New Orleans in 2017–2018 applied to other locations and conditions. We list the most-important conditions in the following paragraphs, including having an allowance for a burn-in period, bringing in industry partners to create a demand-driven curriculum, casting a wide recruiting net, incorporating hands-on learning as part of the curriculum where possible, and potentially using tests of basic literacy and numeracy to select candidates for training.

Given the poor cost-benefit results early in the program and the turnaround to positive returns following these initially poor results, time should be built into similar training programs for learning. Our results strongly suggest that the program improved after the first few cohorts of training. If the program had been evaluated simply on these initial programs, it would have been viewed as a very ineffective intervention. The city and training providers needed to learn, through trial and error, the best approaches for screening and predicting participant success; this, in turn, produced positive economic results. Implementers should be patient with these types of interventions and potentially start with smaller training cohorts for the first few waves as they figure out what relationships and programs are required to move forward.

Be flexible, and consider employer needs in creating workforce education and training programs. There are potential lessons to be learned from the change of sectors; i.e., dropping the energy sector and bringing on the health care and IT sectors. The energy sector was first considered to be a viable target industry for OWD to partner with when local firms in the energy sector (specifically, the oil and natural gas industry) had high demand for labor, given high oil prices. However, in 2015 and 2016 there was a drop in oil prices (after the WIF proposal was submitted but before the program began) that decreased the industry's interest in hiring. Sector-specific demand-driven programs such as these might always be sensitive to changes in demand exogenous to the firms. Any job training program should therefore be flexible enough to respond to these changes in a timely manner, as well as train candidates in skills that will be useful across multiple industries. We are not sure whether this means that the original and current sectors were chosen "correctly." Sectors were chosen based on perceived interest from the firms as determined by OWD interactions with industry points of contact.

Where feasible, incorporate hands-on practice and classroom instruction. The provision of fully online training to the program population enrolled in the IT pathway is potentially concerning. Though online programs have many benefits, this mode of instruction might not have been the most effective for a vulnerable population that might have multiple competing demands and limited professional experience. Blended approaches to instruction might be a better option because they have the potential to address nontraditional students with unique needs during the part of instruction that occurs in class. The class becomes part of the students' routines, and students are able to get immediate responses to their questions and concerns. Furthermore, trainees in focus groups frequently cited the desire to have more hands-on experience in their coursework, though around 75 percent of telephone survey respondents agreed or strongly agreed that the trainer balanced lectures with hands-on activities.

Creating strong and sustainable partnerships between government and nongovernment entities can be challenging. The ability to build such partnerships is affected by funding constraints and changes in the economic and political contexts in which the partnerships are embedded. For example, the partnership with employers in the hospitality industry appears to have been based on a misunderstanding regarding the willingness of these employers to refer current employees for training. Firms in the energy sector that showed initial interest in partnering in this effort withdrew their commitments due to the economic implications they felt as a result of the drop in oil prices. Similarly, many cultural partners that were interested in being partners in the Career Pathways program were unable to do so because there were not adequate funds for compensation, and those that were involved did not ultimately provide a viable pathway for continued recruitment and screening. Findings also suggest that the partnerships were loosely built and very few of them were formalized. This design could have been intentional.

When confronted with challenges, OWD acted strategically in how it involved employers, allowing the business sector to define its needs and how it developed a demand-driven curriculum and to participate in hiring when possible. OWD coordinated its efforts around the program, but there were no truly collaborative partnerships in which partners worked together to define common goals, share information, and participate in decisionmaking. This limited effectiveness of the collaboration might have been due to a number of reasons, such as lack of true employer labor demand, lack of employer capacity to help, missteps or insufficient outreach by OWD in these interactions, or evidence that these collaborations are unhelpful in training development and execution. Overall, OWD responded effectively to lessons learned: the current recruitment is sufficiently large and the screening seems to be, if nothing else, working to send some to the potential trainee pool and remaining individuals elsewhere to receive other help from OWD.

Plan job training programs that have participation from industry in curriculum design and capitalized commitments to follow-up, but be flexible and agile enough to make changes in industry partners as needed. We believe that the demand-driven aspect of the training program was critical to its success; the connections with local firms allowed OWD the agility to switch pathways after energy sector demand dried up. However, more could have been done in the training to connect workers with local firms. While on-the-job training funds were allocated, these were severely underutilized. One of the most successful models employed out of the cohorts was the one trained by Oschner, more directly connecting training with potential employers. The Oschner model is not necessarily reproducible in all cases, but local WIBs can form meaningful industry partnerships and buy-in that allow for post-training introductions and support. Furthermore, while the initial partnership involved firms in the energy sector, when oil prices decreased and demand for energy-sector trainees diminished, OWD was agile enough to switch industry partners, which was likely important to the success of the program.

Screening could improve training completion and better outcomes, though more research is necessary to understand which profiling tool would have the best outcome. We learned that the initial plans to use hospitality firms and community partners to screen did not work—hospitality firms withdrew for fear of losing their best workers, and community partners were unlikely to impose a binding screening, instead recommending everyone they encountered during the screening process. We also found no evidence that the eventual interview score was effective in identifying those more likely to complete training or screen those with the highest treatment effects. Instead, it seems that the TABE test of basic literacy and numeracy scores has the best potential characteristics. Additional research is required to parse how the treatment effects (and control group results) differ, depending on which profiling tool the cohort is exposed to, as well as how combinations of the tools might improve treatment assignment.

These job training programs are effective for workers who are more than 35 years old, and so could be considered for retraining and midcareer changes. The future for older workers who are displaced due to exogenous factors, such as outsourcing or technological innovation, is often a cause for concern—especially outcomes for low-income older workers. However, we found that these populations had larger treatment effects, suggesting that a part-time medium-skill training of two to four months in a high-demand area could offer a meaningful solution to retraining such workers over 35 years old and providing them with skills that can improve their outcomes.

Make sure nonemployment benefits are included when considering the value of programs. We found improvements in job satisfaction from training. While we did not find statistically significant effects on crime, our study did suggest that future research might benefit from evaluating the impact of job training programs on arrests. Most evaluations of these job training programs would have been limited to employment and earnings, and would have missed gains from the program in these other dimensions.

Increasing the size of training to hundreds of individuals in the city did not seem to be a problem, but it is unclear what more-extensive scaling would yield. The program succeeded even as additional trainers and training cohorts were added on. This is encouraging with respect to the scalability of these types of programs in any given city. However, training providers should be carefully vetted and monitored, and target industries require buy-in, so there would be a definite ceiling on the scalability of this program. Even though we found mixed evidence on the prescreening efforts with regard to outcomes, our best evidence from this study suggests that leveraging the TABE is beneficial for selecting individuals qualified for training, and this would put another limit on the number of trainees. WIBs should use these tests not to decide which individuals to assist, but to target appropriate assistance decisions. Those with sufficiently high TABE scores, for example, should be routed toward these types of training programs, while those with TABE scores below the relevant threshold should be routed to alternative programs and assistance from the WIB.

Further work is needed in several areas surrounding this job training. For example, we would like to further investigate the role of credentialing, which trainees felt was important. We also need to better understand the optimal collection of prescreening profiling tools. However, this study strongly suggests that there is space in our public policy for job training programs aimed at low-income workers, if such a program is well designed and targeted.

Implementation Analysis Methodology

The evaluation looks at the key steps in the implementation of the project, including the factors that facilitate or impede executing the logic model presented in Chapter 1. To do this, we conducted a process evaluation (implementation study). A process evaluation is conducted to document and analyze the early development and implementation of a program or intervention, assessing whether and how well services are delivered as intended or planned (Wholey, Hatry, and Newcomer, 2010; Rossi et al., 2004; Patton, 2001). We used the logic model as a guiding template and touchstone for the process evaluation; we reviewed how program activities were implemented and documented that process and the progress of the initiative as a whole. In a process evaluation, findings can support ongoing revisions to policies. Thus, we used the findings from the process evaluation to continually identify areas of strength and areas needing improvement to enable the training providers and OWD to understand whether the project was working in a way that would promote the intended outcomes and whether this could be scalable to other sectors (Wholey, Hatry, and Newcomer, 2010; Rossi et al., 2004). The findings from the process evaluation also provided contextual information to explain results from the quantitative outcomes and cost-effectiveness analyses.

To assess the implementation of Career Pathways, we identified the original design features of the program, juxtaposing those features with the information from the interviews and focus groups. The information then was synthesized qualitatively to assess whether each of the three design features were implemented as intended or whether adjustments were made and why.

Outcome Analysis Methodology

B.1. Randomization

For each training cohort, interested individuals who passed the screening mechanism, signed the consent forms to participate in our study, and filled out the baseline survey entered into the randomization pool for that cohort. When the recruitment for a given cohort was completed, OWD would provide us a list of all of the eligible candidates for that training cohort, along with their background surveys. We eliminated veterans from the lottery because they were guaranteed participation in the training per DOL protocols. We generated a set of four binary variables for each individual: gender (male or female), employment status (working or not working), annual income (more or less than $5,000), and age (younger or older than 35 years old). From these, we created 16 gender-by-employment-by-income-by-age strata cells. If any of the 16 cells had only one person in it, we pooled that cell with the closest matching cell, according to a preprogrammed ordering of proximity (e.g., male, low-income, unemployed, and young individuals would be pooled with male, low-income, unemployed, and older individuals). Once there were no singleton cells, each person was assigned a random number and ordered by that number within each stratum, with half assigned treatment and half assigned control. As some strata cells had an odd number of persons within the cell, we randomly ordered the odd strata groups and alternated between picking one more or one less person to be assigned treatment than control for each consecutive group. We stratified along these dimensions to improve the likelihood of balance—or baseline similarity and thus comparability—between control and treatment groups.

B.2. Baseline Equivalence

We test baseline equivalence of the treatment and control groups in terms of sociodemographic characteristics reported at the baseline and the profiling tools described in Table B.1. We define equivalence for a given variable as an effect size less than 0.20; that is, the difference between the treatment and control means for that variable is less than 20 percent of the pooled standard deviation. This is equivalent to Cohen's (1988) threshold for a small effect, and is more conservative than the 0.25 threshold used by U.S. Department of Education's What Works Clearinghouse. The equivalence in sociodemographic characteristics (i.e., the first four variables in Table B.1: gender, age, employment, annual income above $5,000) was expected, as we used block randomization within the cells defined by the intersection of the variables, as described previously. Notably, we also find balance on the profiling tool scores. The randomization achieved equivalence in the baseline outcomes before randomization (and thus, before training)— average employment, earnings, job stability, arrest rates, and screening test scores—which we did not stratify for randomization. The one exception is the Wonderlic score, a common test of pre-employment capability that has an effect size of 0.29. However, we note that this difference is not statistically significant at even the 10-percent level, and that this is for the smaller subsample of individuals who were administered the Wonderlic and had scores transmitted to RAND. Note that we had some missing interview scores and TABE scores for some individuals who should have had these scores present, as well as legitimate cases where the profiling tool was not used for a given cohort.

Table B.1
Baseline Equivalence Results

	Control	Treatment	Difference	P-value from T-Test	Effect Size
% male	0.55	0.60	−0.05	0.64	0.10
% older (≥ 35 years old)	0.51	0.59	−0.08	0.12	0.16
% employed	0.53	0.54	0.00	0.94	0.01
% income above $5,000	0.60	0.64	−0.04	0.51	0.08
Average pre-employment	0.60	0.62	−0.01	0.78	0.03
Average pre-earnings	3526	3584	−58	0.91	0.01
Arrested before randomization	0.40	0.43	−0.03	0.46	0.06
Maximum job tenure	3.86	3.55	0.31	0.36	0.11
TABE	7.37	7.71	−0.34	0.49	0.17
Wonderlic	22.23	21.10	1.13	0.26	0.29
Interview score	80.54	81.90	−1.36	0.58	0.17

NOTE: This analysis includes only cohorts used in the analysis. That is, it includes only cohorts with post-training earnings data and with information on training dates received from the training provider. Numbers are unweighted and unadjusted.

B.3. Sampling Design, Inclusion Criteria, Attrition, and Weighting

As mentioned above, we exclude veterans from the analysis because they were not randomized but were all assigned to the treatment per DOL policy. Furthermore, we include only individuals for whom we have post-training outcomes. For the employment and earnings analysis, this means that their assigned cohort finished training prior to June 30, 2018 (so that we have at least one post-training quarter of data from LWC, given our last available data are from the third quarter of 2018). For the crime outcome, we use all participants because we have crime data through April 2019, after all cohorts had finished training. Analyses of telephone survey data also used all cohorts for which we had at least one respondent, as none were excluded because their training had not ended or for any other reason. The inclusion or exclusion of each cohort is shown in Table 2.2. We had attrition from the telephone survey sample due to either not having up-to-date contact information or nonresponsiveness; this is discussed in the following subsection. We also had some individuals whose Social Security numbers did not match in the LWC data set for any quarter of data in the 2014–2018 data range. This could happen for one of at least four reasons:

- The person never worked in Louisiana during that time and thus should be considered unemployed in our data.
- The person could have worked only "under the table" or for excludable jobs that would not be reported in LWC data, in which case employment outcomes should be considered missing in our data (not knowing their earnings or employment).
- The person could have left Louisiana and had earnings in other states, and thus earnings should be considered zero (as we are investigating earnings in Louisiana only).
- The person could have entered the incorrect Social Security number, in which case we should consider the individual as missing.

Not knowing which of the four cases or combination thereof any individual was, we coded each of these persons as missing and corrected for this using nonresponse weights.

Similarly, for the crime outcome, we could not tell whether someone was missing these data because they left New Orleans or did not commit any crimes. In the face of this missing information, we defined the outcome implicitly in terms of the sample (i.e., employment in Louisiana or arrests in Orleans Parish) so we set the missing records for these outcomes to zero, with the exception of individuals not located in LWC data by Social Security number (see previous), which we set as missing in the crime data. If the treatment individuals were more (less) likely to leave the state or Orleans Parish than the control individuals, this would lead to under (over) estimation of the treatment effects (i.e., in any geography) for employment and earnings by assuming that they are unemployed, and over (under) estimation of the full treatment effects for arrests by assuming they did not get arrested.

Table B.2 presents the total number of participants in the program. 509 nonveteran individuals consented to participate in the study. As discussed in Chapter 2, the program was set up so that a person assigned to be in the control group for a given cohort could enter into a later randomization cohort; the person could be assigned to the treatment group and receive training later, though they were not necessarily encouraged to do so by OWD above and beyond what any individual who walked in to a JOB1 center would receive, nor were they provided an explicit path into the later cohort. This represented business as usual for the control group (they could receive later benefits from the city and JOB1 center); however, the city was instructed to *not* tell the control-assigned individuals that they should enter into new randomization cohorts, only that they could return to the JOB1 center to seek other help. This is represented by the Study ID, a unique identifier given to each person separate for each cohort they might be in. Thus, for the persons who are in four different cohorts (the maximum value for a small selection of individuals who were randomized into control groups three times, and then finally into the treatment group in their fourth randomization pool), they would have four separate Study IDs. This ability to enter into later randomization cohorts was a requirement of OWD in order to administer the randomization.

There were 42 people who were in more than one randomization cohort because of their being assigned to the control group in the first set of cohorts and re-entering later cohorts' randomization pools. This also represents the reason for the larger number of those only ever assigned treatment (256 individuals) and those only ever assigned control (211 individuals), as such individuals are, by definition, assigned to the control group first.

The second line of Table B.2 presents the Study IDs in treatment and control. This accounts for the repetition of individuals in more than one cohort by reapplying after being assigned control. Thus, the total number of treated is 256 (those always treated) + 42 repeated individuals = 298, as shown in the second row. The control group grows by more than the 42 because some individuals are in more than one control group, entering the randomization pool up to four times

Table B.2
Number of Program Participants in Outcomes Analysis

	Only Treatment	Only Control	Control and Later Treatment	Total
Number of consented individuals	256	211	42	509
Number of Study IDs	298	281	—	579

(the maximum in our sample). We discuss the methodology for handling these repeats below.

Table B.3 presents the numbers of study participants by outcome. For employment and earnings, we only have 15 of the 24 analysis-sample cohorts with post-treatment earnings data available, given the data timeline from LWC (see Table 2.2). This is also the reason for the smaller number of individuals in the study. We code any individual with no match in the LWC data as missing, for the reasons described above. This accounts for approximately 8 percent of the sample and is equal between control and treatment groups.

Table B.3 also reports the number of clusters used for calculating the standard errors. As described later, we defined clusters at the cohort level for the treatment group (as outcomes may be correlated with each other) and at the individual level for the control group (given that we expect no correlation in outcomes for control persons who happened to be in the same randomization cohort). Table 4.3 shows that we have 172 clusters for the analysis of employment and earnings.

For the analysis of the effects on crime, we have a large sample covering all cohorts (comparing the sample of those for whom we have post-training data in the arrest file with those in Table B.2) as we acquired administrative data on arrests from the New Orleans Police Department for all individuals in the study. As a result, we have crime data for 24 cohorts and 252 clusters. However, we assume that all individuals who did not match Social Security numbers in the LWC employment data are also missing for the arrest data. This is supported by the fact that none of these Social Security numbers match any arrest records, before or after training, which would be very unlikely given

Table B.3
Samples and Responses by Outcome

		Employment and Earnings	Crime	Job Satisfaction
Potential numbers given data frame	Treatment	239	298	298
	Control	189	278	278
	T/C ratio	1.26	1.07	1.07
Available in data	Treatment	222	273	76
	Control	173	252	26
	T/C ratio	1.28	1.08	2.92
Response rates	Treatment	93%	92%	26%
	Control	92%	91%	9%
Number of cohorts		15	24	21
Number of clusters	Treatment	15	24	21
	Control	157	228	26
	Total	172	252	47

that, overall, around 40 percent of participants had been arrested at some point in their lives before training.

For the analysis of job satisfaction, the overall response rate for the phone survey was around 20 percent, with the treatment group more than double the response rate of the control group. The nonresponses are due either to not having correct or updated contact information for study members or because individuals did not respond to our repeated attempts to survey them.[1] We found a higher rate of responses to the

---

[1]   Another important thing to note is that we do not have a full definition of treatment status for job satisfaction, given that we are unable to always reliably match on names. We use treatment assignment from our baseline surveys whenever there is a clean merge on the participant's name with the analytic data file (i.e., the randomization data file). However, some persons were not able to merge, and for them we use their survey response to the question of whether they participated in the Career Pathways program. We do not rely solely on this latter measure because there are incorrect responses to this question based on the sample of individuals that do merge. To be safe, for any individual who did merge, we used the true

telephone survey among the treated individuals than among control individuals, though the rates of response are below 30 percent for even the treatment group. One reason for the lower response rate for the control group is because we could not field surveys to some of the repeaters during the time they were in the control but before joining the treatment group. Another is that, despite the financial incentives to reply, control persons may feel less obligated to reply because they were not trained.

To correct for missingness in each of the data sets, as discussed previously, we use inverse probability weights for nonresponse. To do so, for any outcome and data set, we first fit a logistic regression of nonmissing indicators onto the person's treatment status and the four randomization strata of baseline age, sex, income, and employment status. Using this fitted regression, we predict the probability of being a nonmissing response and generate the regression weights as the inverse of this predicted probability. Thus, individuals who are often missing covariates will have a lower prediction of being nonmissing, which when inverted will yield a larger weight to account for the persons who are similar and are missing data.

B.4. Statistical Methods

We measure the effect of ITT, or assignment to training status, to account for incomplete participation in training or noncompliance with random assignment (Huber, 2012; Imbens and Rubin, 1997). This is the policy-relevant estimator, because it provides the average effect over all eligible individuals, allowing for the fact that there will be imperfect compliance with random assignment. We also estimate the local average treatment effect for those who attend at least one training class through instrumenting the attendance variable with treatment status.

We clustered the standard errors to reflect expected intraclass correlations. We did so using multilevel clustering. Specifically, each

---

treatment status, while for anyone who did not merge, we used their response to the participation in the Career Pathways program.

person assigned treatment is assigned to a cluster given by their training cohort (of which there are up to 24, depending on the model), while each control person is assigned his or her own cluster because we do not expect there to be any correlation in a control person's outcomes with any other control person, but we do expect correlation within individuals across time and across cohorts if they are in more than one cohort. That is, the clustering allows but does not require correlation across observations of a person in multiple cohorts while in the control group but assumes the more conservative cohort-level clustering once they are in a treatment group. We also cluster at the individual level across all individuals to account for repeated observations per treated persons that will have correlation. Given the imbalance of cluster size and the small fraction of clusters that are treated given this approach, we adjust p-values using wild bootstrap clusters (Roodman et al., 2018).

A person may be in more than one cohort. To account for this, we generate Study IDs, which are unique to each person within a training cohort but not necessarily across cohorts for those who enter more than one randomization cohort (see Table B.2 and the surrounding discussion for more on this). If a person enters a later cohort, they are assigned a second Study ID when they enter the new cohort (whether they are a treatment assignment or control again). They will have a separate set of quarterly observations for this new Study ID running from after the new randomization date until the third quarter of 2018, including lagged outcomes that are calculated with respect to the randomization date of their new cohort. If they are randomized into the control group of their new cohort, they have the opportunity to enter yet another cohort at a later date, get assigned another Study ID, and contribute more records to the regression. As mentioned in Chapter Two, the most cohorts entered by any individual was four.

The only time that an individual's quarterly observations are truncated prior to the third quarter of 2018 are if the individual enters a new cohort and is randomized into the treatment group. For such a person, we included quarterly observations for all of his or her previous cohorts, truncated at the date he or she was randomized into treatment, as well as a set of quarterly records with a new Study ID for the cohort in which he or she was treated.

In addition to the ITT effects, we estimate the local average treatment effect for attending treatment at least once (Imbens and Angrist, 1994). In these, we use the lottery assignment of being invited to receive training as an instrumental variable for whether the individual attended any training. Given both are binary, this will have the effect of scaling the treatment effect up (in absolute value), depending on the level of program attendance.

As discussed in the research questions in Chapter 1.5, we designate each analysis either confirmatory or exploratory. *Confirmatory analysis* is that which seeks to directly test a hypothesis and provide causal evidence of whether that hypothesis is true or not, and requires the strongest identification; *exploratory analysis* is used to generate hypotheses—for example, for future research. To account for our testing multiple hypotheses within a domain in confirmatory analysis, we use Benjamini and Hochberg (1995) false discovery rate corrections. In classifying domains for the multiple hypothesis corrections, we did our best to follow the advice in Schochet (2008). First, we did correction only for estimators classified as confirmatory. Second, we considered outcomes reflecting separate aspects of the labor market as separate domains. As stated in Schochet, "Outcome domains should be delineated using theory or a conceptual framework that relates the program or intervention to the outcomes. The domains should reflect key clusters of constructs represented by the central research questions of the study" (Schochet, 2008, p. 4). We put each outcome into a separate domain, as we believe they are each evaluating a different aspect of the potential success of the program. We also separate into different domains *within outcome* according to the research question, representing our interpretation of the last sentence of the prior quote. Thus, the question of the impact of training on earnings is a different research question and, in our minds a different domain from the heterogeneity of returns to training across different demographic groups. We further separate into domains the 2016 cohorts and 2017 and later cohorts, as we believe these are two fundamentally different periods of time (the burn-in period and the fully realized program period). We put ITT and 2SLS analyses in the same domain, reflecting that they are measuring the same research question, outcome, and underlying model of action. Because of this, there are no adjustments across tables or figures in this report, but for confirmatory analysis, there is always some correction within a table, as we have noted in the note on each table.

As we look at several outcomes and models, we describe each in detail.

B.4.1. Models for Chapter 4.1

In Chapter 4.1, we investigate the trends in program attendance, completion, and credentialing. Table 4.1 and Figure 4.1 are raw statistics over the defined populations. Table 4.2 is based on a regression where we keep one observation per Study ID assigned treatment status. Equation B.1 presents the regression used. ε_{ic} is the unobserved error term.

$$Y_{ic} = \alpha + \beta\, StartQ_c + \varepsilon_{ic}$$

Y_{ic} represents a set of three dependent variables, each an indicator for whether individual i in cohort c: (1) attended training at least once, (2) completed the first training, and (3) acquired a credential from the training. $StartQ_c$ is a variable that contains the quarter in which an individual's cohort began training, measured in years. β is the coefficient reported in Table 4.2, and measures how a one-year difference in the start of training (e.g., a cohort that began in the fourth quarter of 2017 instead of the fourth quarter of 2016) is related to changes in the outcomes. This analysis is exploratory.

Table 4.3 provides an estimator for how characteristics of the trainees are related to the probability of attendance and completion. Specifically, it is based on equation B.2, where we again keep one observation per Study ID.

$$Y_{ic} = \alpha + S_i \beta + \psi_c + \varepsilon_{ic}$$

Y_{ic} represents a set of three dependent variables, each an indicator for whether individual i in cohort c: (1) attended training at least once,

(2) completed the first training, and (3) acquired a credential from the training. S_i is a vector containing the four randomization strata for individual i: gender, whether he or she is over 35, whether the individual is working at the time he or she applies for training, and whether he or she has annual personal income over \$5,000, each measured at the time of randomization. ψ_c presents cohort fixed effects.

B.4.2. Models for Chapter 4.2
We next present the models associated with Tables 4.4 and 4.5, which look at the impact of training assignment on employment, earnings, and conditional earnings. Equation B.3 presents the model used.

$$Y_{itc} = \alpha + \beta\, Treat_i + \lambda Y_{iB} + X_i\gamma + \psi_c + \phi_t + \varepsilon_{it}$$

Y_{itc} is the dependent variable. It is either a binary variable indicating whether individual i in cohort c is employed in quarter t, or the dollar amount of an individual's earnings from all jobs in quarter t. For each individual, we use all quarters after the end of his or her cohort's training period through the third quarter of 2018, leading to multiple records across time for many individuals. The regression for conditional earnings is the same as the regression for earnings but limits the sample to quarters with nonzero quarterly earnings.

$Treat_i$ (whether or not individual i was selected for training) is the independent variable of interest (with independence ensured through randomization). The covariate Y_{iB} represents the average outcome before the training periods (i.e., at baseline). More specifically, it represents the average quarterly employment rate (for the regressions of employment status) or average quarterly earnings (for the regressions of earnings) from 2.5 years to 0.5 years prior to the randomization.

To reflect the randomization process and increase the precision of our estimates, we additionally control for the baseline characteristics (the fully interacted set of indicator variables for gender, baseline employment status (working or not), baseline annual income (less than or greater than \$5,000), and baseline age (younger or older than 35 years old), captured by X_i, and fixed effects for each cohort, captured by ψ_c. We also include year and quarter fixed effects (φ_t).

We estimate equation B.3 using OLS regression for the ITT model. The TOT model that estimates the effect of attendance on the outcomes estimates a slight modification of equation B.3, given by equation B.4, using 2SLS where attendance in training is instrumented using treatment status.

$$Y_{itc} = \alpha + \beta\,Attend_i + \lambda Y_{iB} + X_i\gamma + \psi_c + \phi_t + \varepsilon_{it}$$

Figure 4.2, which measures the effects on quarterly earnings depending on the starting quarter, is similar to equation B.3, with treatment status and baseline earnings interacted by starting quarter. Specifically, it is given by equation B.5. The summation is across the different starting quarters, with h indexing which quarter a given cohort started in.

$$Y_{itc} =$$
$$\alpha + \sum_h \left(\beta_h Treat_i + \lambda_h Y_{iB} + h\right) \times 1\left(StartQ_h = c\right) + X_i\gamma$$
$$+\psi_c + \phi_t + \varepsilon_{it}$$

Figure 4.3 measures how the treatment effect changes depending on how many quarters have elapsed since the end of training. It, too, is a modification of equation B.3 for earnings, and is given by equation B.6. The summation is across which quarter after the end of training the observation is in, with s indexing the quarter.

$$Y_{itc} = \alpha + \sum_s \beta_s Treat_i \times 1\left(s = t\right) + X_i\gamma + \psi_c + \phi_s + \varepsilon_{it}$$

Table 4.4 examines how the effects on employment status and earnings differ depending on which pathway the cohort was in, using a simple interaction of treatment status and cohort. This is estimated by equation B.7, where we look at the pathways for AM, health care, or IT, with the pathway indexed by h.

$$Y_{itc} = \alpha + \sum_{h=AM,IT,H} \beta_h Treat_i \times 1\left(c \in h\right) + \lambda Y_{iB} + X_i \gamma + \psi_c + \phi_t + \varepsilon_i$$

Figure 4.5 estimates the effects by different subgroups, and does so by interacting treatment status with the subgroups. This is done separately for each subgroup (e.g., a separate regression investigating the differences by gender from the regression investigating the differences by age), as shown in equation B.8, where X_{pi} is the scalar for the pth variable investigated: gender, age, baseline employment status, and baseline earnings.

$$Y_{itc} = \alpha + \sum_{s=0,1} \beta_s Treat_i \times 1\left(X_{pi} = s\right) + \lambda Y_{iB} + X_i \gamma + \psi_c + \phi_t + \varepsilon_{it}$$

Table 4.6 presents the likelihood of working in the target industries.

$$Emp.Ind.H_{itc} = \alpha + \beta Treat_i + \lambda WorkedH_i + X_i\gamma + \psi_c + \phi_t + \varepsilon_{it}$$

Here, $Emp.Ind.H_{itc}$ is an indicator for the individual working in industry H (which is tested separately for each of the three target industries). $Worked\ H_i$ is an indicator for having worked in industry H in the four years prior to the start of training. Both take the value of zero (and not missing) when an individual is not working. We do this separately for the sample of all individuals and for those in cohorts targeting industry H.

B.4.3. Models for Chapter 4.3

Chapter 4.3.1 investigates the impact of training on job duration. For this, we estimate a Cox model, with one observation per job per Study

ID in the post-training period. We use a Cox model here because it is very common for jobs to end during the data period, and because there is a more complicated pattern of censored data, with jobs starting at very different times that are not finished when the data sample ends. We evaluate each job that is held after the start of training for each individual. The model is represented by equation B.10, where $h_{icj}(t)$ is an indicator for still having a job t quarters after starting job j, $h_0(t)$ is the baseline hazard function, and $HadAtStart_{ij}$ is an indicator for individual i holding job j at the start of training. We again tested a linear model for comparison, and it yielded very similar results.

$$h_{icj}(t) = h_0(t) \exp\left(\beta Treat_i + X_i\gamma + \delta HadAtStart + \psi_c\right)$$

Chapter 4.3.2 investigates the impact of training on job satisfaction. The outcome is the measure of job satisfaction (on a 0 to 3 scale) from the telephone surveys. Equation B.11 presents the model for Table 4.8, estimated using OLS. The sample is limited to individuals who had a job at the time of the survey (because they were the only ones asked about how satisfied they were with their jobs). They were asked either in an initial survey ($t = 1$) or in a follow-up survey approximately six months later ($t = 2$). Here, we do not control for the fully interacted 16 cells of the randomization strata but the four marginal strata (baseline gender, age over 35, working status, and income). We also do not control for cohort fixed effects. We do not control for these two (as we do in the other models) because of the much smaller sample size.

$$Satis_{it} = \alpha + \beta Treat_i + S_i\delta + \phi_t + \varepsilon_{it}$$

Figure 4.6 is similar, separately estimating the effect depending on how strongly the treated respondents reported agreeing that training helped them either find a better job or in their current job (measured by $Helped_{it}$). Given that this is unobserved for control persons, and for better comparisons, we impute the *Helped*$_{it}$ variable for control persons. We do so by fitting an ordered logistic regression of the response to *Helped*$_{it}$ on their marginal strata S_i and the period (first survey after training or the follow-up survey). We do this regression only on the sample of treated persons who responded to the survey and this question, and then predict the probabilities of answering each response (strongly agree, agree, disagree, strongly disagree) using these estimated coefficients for the control group. For each individual, we then assign as the imputed response to *Helped*$_{it}$ the value of the four levels of agreement that has the highest predicted probability. We replace the missing values of *Helped*$_{it}$ with these imputed values for the sample of control persons who answered the job satisfaction question (the dependent variable). We then estimate equation B.12. Note that this requires more assumptions than are made in the other analyses because of this imputation. We are making a missing at random (conditional on the covariates used) assumption that implies that, conditional on these covariates, there are no remaining unobserved confounders for the control group that are jointly related to the true probability of being in one of these subgroups (e.g., if they had treatment, then how strongly they would agree it helped them with their job) and the outcome of job satisfaction. We acknowledge that this may be a strong assumption in this case; hence, we deem this an exploratory analysis that can shed some light into the potential differences in the observed differences in job satisfaction between the treatment and control group.

$$Satis_{it} = \alpha + \sum\nolimits_{s=1,2,3,4} \beta Treat_i \times 1 \left(Helped_{it} = s \right) + S_i \delta + \phi_t + \varepsilon_{it}$$

We next discuss the methodology for Chapter 4.3.3, which looks at the impact on arrests. For these analyses of crime, we keep one observation per Study ID (i.e., we do not use each quarter record per Study ID). Equation B.13 presents this model, in which *arrested*$_i$ is an indicator of being arrested after the start of the individual's cohort started training, *base arrest*$_i$ is an indicator for being arrested ever before the start of training, and *time*$_i$ is a measure in days converted to years from the start of training until April 25, 2019, when we received the data draw from the NOPD. This is to account for the fact that earlier cohorts had a longer period in which they could have been arrested after the start of training. The rest of the parameters are as defined above. We also use a Cox proportional hazards model for time until arrest, which allows for right-censored data, and found the same basic results from that analysis. We opted not to use the Cox model because there was no existing software for implementing the wild bootstrap clustered methodology with the Cox model.

$$arrested_i =$$
$$\alpha + \beta\,Treat_i + \lambda\,basearrest_i + \delta\,time_i$$
$$+\theta\,time_i \times Treat_i + X_{it}\gamma + \psi_c + \varepsilon_{it}$$

We also test the model for different demographic subgroups for Figure 4.7, shown in equation B.14. This is done separately for each subgroup (e.g., a separate regression investigating the differences by gender from the regression investigating the differences by age), as shown in equation B.14, where X_{pi} is the scalar for the variable investigated: gender, age, baseline employment status, and baseline earnings.

$$Y_{ic} = \alpha + \sum_{s=0,1} \beta_s\,Treat_i \times 1\left(X_{pi} = s\right) +$$
$$\lambda\,basearrest_i + \delta\,time_i + \theta\,time_i \times Treat_i$$
$$+X_i\gamma + \psi_c + \varepsilon_{it}$$

B.4.4. Models for Chapter 4.4

Chapter 4.4 presents results for the analysis around the profiling tools. We first examine the effect of the profiling tool scores on the outcomes of attendance, completion, and credentialing, as shown in Table 4.10. This is estimated using equation B.15. As is done for the job satisfaction regressions, we use the four marginal strata instead of the fully interacted 16 cells of X_i. *Profile$_i$* is the profiling tool scores, as shown in Table 2.4, and β is the coefficients of interest reported in Table 2.4.

$$Y_{ic} = \alpha + \beta \; Pr \; ofile_i + S_i\gamma + \psi_c + \varepsilon_{it}$$

For estimating screening versus creaming as shown in Table 4.11, we estimate equation B.16 for each examined profiling tool score. β_2 measures the extent of creaming given the score, as it is how much the outcome changes with an improvement in the score for the control group. β_3 is the measure of screening, or how much the treatment effect itself improves for an increase in the profiling tool score. The desire is to have a large and positive β_3, so that one is selecting individuals who will benefit the most from training, while potentially minimizing (negative and large) β_2 so as to anti-cream, or select individuals who would not fare as well without the training. Y_{itc} looks at the outcomes of employment status and quarterly earnings.

$$Y_{itc} = \alpha + \beta_1 Treat_i + \beta_2 \; Pr \; ofile_i + $$
$$\beta_3 Treat_i \times Pr \; ofile_i + X_i\gamma + \phi_t + \psi_c + \varepsilon_{it}$$

B.4.5. Model for Chapter 4.5

We also investigate the effect that peers have on outcomes (as reported in Figure 4.8); that is, how the quality of other individuals in a cohort, as measured by various profiling tool scores, impacts the employment and earnings outcomes of individuals. To do so, we estimate equation B.17 for just one group at a time, either the treatment group or the control group. *Profile$_{-lc}$* is the average profiling tool score for all other persons in individual 's cohort, and β_2 is our estimate of the effect of a person's cohort peers.

$$Y_{itc} = \alpha + \beta_1 \; Pr \; ofile_i + \beta_2 \; Pr \; ofile_{-lc} + X_{it}\gamma + \phi_t + \varepsilon_{it}$$

B.5. Threats to Validity

The validity of the RCT analysis depends on our ability to obtain outcome data from all members of the treatment and control groups. Fortunately, most of our outcome data come from administrative data sources. Therefore, we have over 90 percent of employment and earnings outcomes data on all RCT subjects that accurately reported their Social Security number and remain in Louisiana. We have complete arrests outcomes data for arrests in Orleans Parish for all individuals for whom we have LWC data. We could be underrepresenting employment or arrests if some subjects leave the area to work or commit crimes. However, we have no *a priori* reason to expect this to be systematically different between the treatment and control subjects. While the relatively transient nature of the New Orleans population makes this something of a concern, this is offset by the fact that New Orleans is not on the state boundary (as are many big cities) and Orleans Parish makes up a large portion of the metropolitan area population.

We do, on the other hand, lose many subjects to survey follow-up in the job satisfaction analysis. We attempted to minimize this loss by providing financial incentives for survey-takers, but we still ended up with about a 20-percent response rate for the control group, and a much higher response rate for treated persons.

We handle missing data throughout by implementing survey nonmissing weights using inverse probability weights, as described in Chapter B.3. This approach provides consistent estimates if missingness was random, conditional on baseline characteristics.

External validity: Even if we have strong internal validity through randomization, we cannot necessarily claim that these results would hold in other settings. This was a more serious concern for the originally proposed study design, in which the training plan relied on the unique seasonal hospitality and leisure industry and the presence of community partners, such as the Social Aid and Pleasure Clubs. However, as implemented, the program is much more easily replicated in any metropolitan area. Local WIBs and cities can implement their own screening tools and use local firms to design the curriculum. However, as is true in any city, the New Orleans labor market has unique features that could limit the generalizability of our findings.

Heterogeneous effects: One of the strengths of this initiative—variation in training providers and provided skills—also leads to challenges in estimating the overall impact. We have adequate power to estimate the average impact of the initiative, but not to precisely estimate the impact of individual training programs or providers, and we are left with an overall estimate that is composed of several different training providers and programs that are at times quite different. Furthermore, our lack of power at the cohort or provider level makes it difficult to provide strong evidence about which provider or trainee features lead to a large positive impact.

Cost-Benefit Study Methodology

The evaluation is only able to directly estimate program benefits up to one to two years post-training, and assumes that the later benefits will be equal to the average benefits in the first year and a half. Furthermore, less data is available to analyze the later cohorts, some of which ended training after the end of our LWC data-collection period. Additional assumptions are needed to calculate the lifetime benefits of the training. A key factor in the calculation of lifetime earnings is determining what assumption to make regarding how the earnings gap changes over time. While the Hollenbeck (2012) study shows a decrease in the earnings gap between treatment and control groups over time and therefore uses a decay rate to account for this convergence, the analysis of this training program does not show a similar decrease (see Figure 4.3 and the surrounding discussion). Because the number of quarters of data collected post-treatment is not very large, it would be difficult to draw any conclusions suggesting this gap would continue to increase at a constant rate. Therefore, to be conservative in the estimate of the benefits from earnings, we assume that the absolute dollar amount gap will remain constant into the future.

In order to estimate the cost of the program per trainee, we employed the Resource Cost Model (RCM) approach (Levin and McEwan, 2000). RCM assesses costs by viewing the total cost as an aggregation of the costs of all of the inputs—or resources—employed in the program. We collected all direct costs reported on itemized budgets from program implementation, with indirect or unreported costs gathered through in-person interviews and follow-up questionnaires with members of OWD government and contractor staff, source and target firms, and training providers.

The in-person interviews helped provide context for the costs, including the types of activities conducted with the various resources expended. Costs are categorized into the activities they supported (e.g., screening, outreach). All costs are adjusted for inflation using the Consumer Price Index and presented in 2018 dollars.

To use best practices and leverage prior work, we modified existing RCM interview templates based on prior related RAND research (Schwartz and Karoly, 2011). The interviews served two major functions. First, they allowed the organizations to report all indirect or nonmonetary costs (such as volunteer work and the use of facilities) and served as a prompt for each group to consider more-obscure resources as costs. Second, the interviews enabled the groups to accurately identify and communicate fractional contributions, such as the number of hours that management spent on the pipeline project, which could then be added to the total expenditure.

Given the strong possibility of large start-up costs in establishing such a job training program, we analyzed the resource costs using the RCM method by year. The in-person interviews were necessary to ensure that the proper time and energy was dedicated to each question and to explain any unclear portions of the interview questions. With annual costs evaluated, the respondents identified which costs were attributable to initiating the program (start-up costs) and which costs were the continuing operational costs of the program.

The following sections describe, in detail, the data sources and methods used to report, estimate, and monetize the costs and benefits of the WIF program. Each section includes a discussion on each component of the cost-benefit analysis, as shown in Table 5.1.

C.1. Benefits

The program benefits we include in this calculation include four components: impact on earnings of receiving the program participation offer, additional fringe benefits received as a result of gaining employment or increasing the level of employment, additional taxes generated (a benefit to the public but a cost to the individual), and benefits from reductions in crime. The following sections explain the methods and data used to estimate these benefits.

C.1.1. Earnings

To estimate the per-participant earnings benefit from the program, the results from ITT regressions were used, as reported in Table 4.5. Details on assumptions and methodologies used in those regressions can be found in that section of the report. We do this for all cohorts, but particularly for the 2017 and later cohorts (where we include the two 2016 cohorts in the costs of the program but estimate the benefits using the post–learning curve results).

C.1.2. Fringe Benefits

Fringe benefits were estimated using data from the BLS. Specifically, the BLS data on "Employer Costs for Employee Compensation – December 2018" was used to estimate a fringe benefit rate (Bureau of Labor Statistics, 2019a). We applied this rate to the quarterly earnings ITT treatment effects and assumed that the estimated fringe benefit rate will persist into the future. Of course, this will likely not be the case in reality, as nonsalary compensation increasingly makes up a larger percentage of total compensation. A further challenge with estimating a reasonable fringe benefit rate is that as an individual's earnings increase, the percentage of their total compensation made up of fringe benefits could go down despite the general overall increase in nonsalary compensation as related to total compensation (which, given the lower income of the population in the study, means we are likely underestimating the value of fringe benefit gains and thus again being conservative). Therefore, there are reasons to believe that these changes could cause the fringe benefit rate to increase or decrease. Holding this rate constant seems like a reasonable assumption based on these uncertainties.

In our model, we are assuming a fringe benefit rate of 38.5 percent. The BLS report shows compensation data for different cross-sections, including by region and by major occupational and industry group.[1] Unfortunately, there was not a breakout by occupation and region, so we examined some rates by region alone and then also by occupational group. The occupational groups showed a fairly large range of job types, so these were found to be less useful for the specific job types in this study. Ultimately, the 38.5 percent rate used in this analysis is the average rate in the West South Central region, which includes the state of Louisiana. Examining some of the occupational groups, which might include the types of jobs included in this study, fringe benefit rates ranged from 35 percent to 42 percent. Because the 38.5 percent rate fell within this range, it seemed reasonable to use this rate for all individuals.

C.1.3. Taxes

There are four types of taxes included in the estimates for tax liabilities for individuals but benefits for the society: payroll taxes, sales or excise taxes, federal income taxes, and state income taxes.

Estimating the impact on participant cost of payroll taxes, including taxes for Social Security and Medicare, is relatively straightforward. The current rate is 7.65 percent of earnings. This rate was used to estimate the future payroll liability for individuals by applying it to the earnings estimates. We assume that this rate will remain steady throughout the estimated period and that all individuals will be employed by other parties (i.e., not self-employed).

Estimating the impact on sales or excise tax is challenging because, unlike the other taxes, the base for which to apply a tax rate is unknown. While we know the state and local sales tax rates for the state of Louisiana, we do not know the consumption expenditures of individuals for which to apply the known rate. We relied on a similar approach that estimates the rate at 4.6 percent for lower-income workers (Hollenbeck and Huang, 2014). The approach compares annual income ranges and data collected on average annual sales and excise taxes for those ranges on a per-individual or per-household basis. Looking at 2017 Louisiana data for both average household income (Federal Reserve Bank of St. Louis, 2018) and average state and local sales tax collections per capita

---

[1]   There are other cross-sections of data; however, they were less useful for this analysis.

(Tax Foundation, 2019), we estimated a sales or excise tax rate relative to income for individuals in Louisiana at 3.6 percent.

Finally, for the impact on federal income tax burden from the participant perspective, we used an effective tax rate of 3.4 percent. This rate was calculated by using 2016 federal income tax return data for the state of Louisiana. Internal Revenue Service data were collected and sorted by various adjusted gross income (AGI) levels (Internal Revenue Service, 2019). The most typical AGI level used in the analysis was a range of $10,000 to $25,000. The total tax liability, as a percentage of total AGI for this group of individuals, was approximately 3.4 percent. This gross method of calculation was chosen to account for the multitude of special tax situations (e.g., Earned Income Tax Credit, which varies by income level and household size) that make it challenging to estimate tax rates at a more granular level.

Finally, for state income taxes, we chose to use a rate of 3 percent. The lowest tax rate in Louisiana is 2 percent on the first $12,500 of net income. The next tax rate is 4 percent on net income between $12,501 and $50,000. Using a similar range assumption as the federal income tax range in the previous paragraph to include earners up to $25,000, we assumed an effective tax rate of 3 percent.

C.1.4. Crime Reduction

As discussed in the outcomes analysis, there is evidence that the gains in employment and earnings contributed to reductions in crime. The costs of crime are well documented and include victim costs (such as medical care, lost earnings, property damage or loss) and public costs (such as police protection, legal and adjudication services, and corrections programs—e.g., incarceration). While we acknowledge these potential benefits, we do not include them in the benefit calculation because it would be difficult to monetize them given the limited specific participant data related to crime (e.g., whether individuals are actually convicted or incarcerated and the exact nature of the crime, which can have significant societal cost differences); also, the net effects of the crime analysis, though showing reductions, were not statistically significant, as discussed in the outcomes analysis chapter.

C.1.5. Transfers

Transfers include components that may represent a benefit to participants but are equally offset by costs to the public. In our cost-benefit study, we specifically analyze four transfers; unemployment compensation, TANF, SNAP, and Medicaid.

C.1.5.1. Unemployment Compensation

Unfortunately, we were unable to collect unemployment compensation data on individuals during the study. Therefore, we are relying on publicly available information and the data we did collect to make assumptions and estimate the potential impact of the program on unemployment compensation on a per-individual basis. Looking at the available earnings data, we used the average baseline earnings as an approximation of historical earnings, which are used in the calculation of an individual's weekly benefit rate (WBR) should the individual become unemployed through no fault of their own. The WBR for Louisiana is then calculated as 4 percent of an average of historical quarterly earnings multiplied by 1.2075. We are assuming that the baseline earnings are roughly indicative of historical earnings. It should be noted that for this calculation, we include all data points in the pre-treatment period, including those of the treatment and control individuals, because at pre-treatment, these groups should be similar, and this allows us to include the largest amount of data available, which increases the accuracy of our estimates. To carry out the calculation, the average baseline quarterly earnings, including all individuals, was $3,096. The WBR is therefore estimated as $149.54. This can be extrapolated to a quarterly amount of $1,943.98.

To estimate the number of participants who may have gained or lost this benefit over the course of the study, we used some gross indicators where participants' baseline salary changed from $0 (presumably unemployed) to any amount greater than $0 (presumably employed) post-treatment. We also considered the opposite situation, where individuals could have lost employment post-treatment. We then calculated the net impact, comparing those who presumably gained employment with those who lost employment from the treatment group, using these gross indicators of employment.

Finally, to qualify for unemployment, the participant must have become unemployed through no fault of their own. They must also be actively looking for work. Without additional data, we assume half of those in our previous net calculation qualify for unemployment compensation. The final amount is calculated by applying this theoretical number of individuals to the assumed quarterly unemployment earnings and dividing by the total number in the treatment group to calculate a dollar amount on a per-participant basis.

C.1.5.2. Temporary Assistance for Needy Families

TANF is the federal government program that provides grants to states as a way to support needy families on a temporary basis. This program is colloquially referred to as "welfare benefits." Each state, in turn, creates specific programs to disburse TANF resources to needy families, according to general guidelines provided by the federal government. The state of Louisiana has several programs that meet the federal government TANF requirements, particularly the Family Independence Temporary Assistance Program (FITAP) and Kinship Care Subsidy Program (KCSP).

We were unable to collect data on individuals receiving FITAP and KCSP benefits over the course of the study. Therefore, we had to rely on public data to make assumptions and estimate the potential impact to these TANF-related benefits on a per-individual basis. First, we used Louisiana state information on eligibility criteria and FITAP and KCSP payout amounts based on income requirements (Louisiana Department of Children and Family Services, undated a; Louisiana Department of Children and Family Services, undated b). Using the income eligibility requirements, we used the earnings data collected on participants, along with telephone survey data on household size, to make assumptions regarding the theoretical number of households and average household size receiving these TANF-related benefits before and after treatment.

With this value, we use the earnings data for participants receiving the treatment to determine who would qualify for this benefit both before and after treatment. On average, as would be expected, fewer participants qualify for both FITAP and KCSP benefits as they gain employment or their earnings increase beyond the maximum to qualify, though the change is marginal. Despite increased earnings on average, many still are below the threshold and qualify for these benefits. There were some cases where those who did not qualify based on pre-treatment earnings did qualify post-treatment.

Using the net decrease for those who qualify for TANF benefits post-treatment, we applied the maximum monthly payout to calculate the decrease in cost. Applying the payout cost to the net number impacted resulted in a total dollar change, which was then divided by the total number of participants in the treatment group to calculate a dollar amount on a per-participant basis. In the analysis, we also time-limited this payout to the maximum number of months, which is sixty months for any individual.

C.1.5.3. Supplemental Nutrition Assistance Program

SNAP, which was formerly known as the Food Stamp Program, is a federal program providing a monthly stipend to low-income people for the purchase of food. We were unable to collect data on individuals receiving SNAP benefits over the course of the study. Therefore, as was the case for TANF, we relied on publicly available information and the data we did collect to estimate the potential impact on SNAP benefits on a per-individual basis. First, we relied on Louisiana state information on eligibility criteria and SNAP payout amounts based on income requirements (Louisiana Department of Children and Family Services, undated c). Using the income eligibility requirements, we used the earnings data collected on participants, along with telephone survey data on household size, to make assumptions regarding the theoretical number of households and average household size receiving the SNAP benefit before and after treatment.

Using Louisiana's Department of Children and Family Services website data for maximum gross monthly income criteria by household size and our participant data and demographic information from telephone surveys, we were able to calculate a weighted average of maximum gross monthly income eligibility standard to account for the average household size of study participants. From our telephone surveys, we were able to estimate how many participants live alone and how many live with other adults (e.g., a spouse or partner) and children, and thus the average size of a household. Based on the data, a rough approximation of household size for those not living alone is four. Using this information, we calculated a weighted average maximum gross monthly income to qualify for SNAP benefits. With this value, we use the earnings data for participants receiving the treatment effect to determine who would qualify for this benefit both before and after treatment. On net, as would be expected, fewer participants qualify for SNAP as they gain employment or their earnings increase beyond the maximum to qualify, though the change is marginal. However, despite increased earnings on average, many still are below the threshold and qualify for SNAP. There were also some cases where those who did not qualify based on pre-treatment earnings did qualify post-treatment.

Using the net decrease for those who qualify for SNAP benefits post-treatment, we applied the weighted average maximum monthly payout to calculate the decrease in cost. As in the maximum gross monthly income standard calculation, the average payout is weighted to account for some individuals living alone (i.e., a household size of one) and another population averaging a household size of four. Applying the payout cost to the net number affected resulted in a total dollar change, which was then divided by the total number of participants in the treatment group to calculate a dollar amount on a per-participant basis.

C.1.5.4. Medicaid

Medicaid is a federal and state program that assists low-income individuals and families with medical care costs. Like the other transfers, participant data on whether individuals receive Medicaid benefits before or after treatment was not collected. We were again left with the method of using available data to estimate the potential pre- and post-treatment impact of potentially being a Medicaid recipient. There are many determining factors that make estimating whether a participant received Medicaid very challenging. For instance, if an individual already receives other welfare benefits (particularly TANF), then recipients are automatically enrolled in Medicaid. There are many Medicaid programs for children, the aged, the disabled, or medically needy families. We cannot ascertain many of these scenarios from the available data on participants in the study. For our purposes, we limit the criteria to Medicaid expansion for adults. In these instances, the income limit is 138 percent of the federal poverty guidelines.

Using data from the Louisiana Department of Health, we determined what the income requirements are for Medicaid recipients and what the average annual payment is for Medicaid recipients. Using the income criteria by household size and our participant data and demographic information from telephone surveys, we were able to calculate a weighted average income eligibility standard adjusted for the average household size of study participants. From our telephone surveys, we could estimate how many participants lived alone and how many lived with other adults (e.g., a spouse or partner) and children, the average size of a household. Based on the data, a rough approximation of household size for those not living alone is four. Using this information, we calculated a weighted average monthly income required to qualify for Medicaid benefits. With this value, we used the earnings data for participants receiving the treatment effect to determine who would qualify for this benefit both before and after treatment. On net, as would be expected, fewer participants qualify for Medicaid as they gain employment or their earnings increase beyond the maximum to qualify, though the change is marginal. It should be noted that there were some cases where those who did not qualify based on pre-treatment earnings did qualify post-treatment.

Using the net decrease for those who qualify for Medicaid benefits post-treatment, we applied the weighted average annual payment per recipient. Applying the payout per-recipient cost to the net number affected resulted in a total dollar change, which was then divided by the total number of participants in the treatment group to calculate a dollar amount on a per-participant basis.

C.2. Costs

There are two costs included in the cost-benefit analysis; forgone earnings and program costs. Forgone earnings represent a cost to participants as they presumably forgo earnings to participate in the training program. Program costs are a cost to the public in the form of subsidies to participants to cover training costs, including tuition and stipends for materials. Additionally, program costs include all government costs to operate the WIF program.

C.2.1. Forgone Earnings

Forgone earnings were estimated using the participant earnings data and conducting OLS regression. Specifically, we did the same regression model as for earnings in the post-training periods, but limited the sample to the training periods. The coefficient on treatment status indicates the expected foregone earnings for participation in training.

C.2.2. Program Costs

Costs are categorized by OWD government costs, OWD contractor costs, and WIF program participant costs in the form of government subsidies to cover training. The government staff's main activity is management of the program. In some cases, these costs could be segregated by activity based on job titles. These were obtained through interviews with key persons and documents provided to us by OWD.

References

Acemoglu, Daron, "Technical Change, Inequality, and the Labor Market," *Journal of Economic Literature*, Vol. 40, No. 1, 2002, pp. 7–72.

Andersson, Fredrik, Harry J. Holzer, Julia I. Lane, David Rosenblum, and Jeffrey Smith, *Does Federally-Funded Job Training Work? Nonexperimental Estimates of WIA Training Impacts Using Longitudinal Data on Workers and Firms*, National Bureau of Economic Research, Working Paper No. 19446, September 2013.

Autor, David H., and David Dorn, "The Growth of Low-Skill Service Jobs and the Polarization of the US Labor Market," *American Economic Review*, Vol. 103, No. 5, August 2013, pp. 1553–1597.

Autor, David H., Lawrence F. Katz, and Melissa S. Kearney, "The Polarization of the U.S. Labor Market," *Measuring and Interpreting Trends in the Economic Inequality*, Vol. 96, No. 2, May 2006, pp. 189–194.

Baird, Matthew, "Labor Supply Estimation Biases from Disregarding Nonwage Benefits," *Economic Inquiry*, Vol. 55, No. 2, April 2017, pp. 1064–1090.

Bell, Stephen H., and Larry L. Orr, "Screening (And Creaming?) Applicants to Job Training Programs: The AFDC Homemaker-Home Health Aide Demonstrations," *Labour Economics*, Vol. 9, No. 2, April 2002, pp. 279–301.

Benjamini, Yoav, and Yosef Hochberg, "Controlling The False Discovery Rate: A Practical and Powerful Approach to Multiple Testing," *Journal of the Royal Statistical Society: Series B (Methodological)*, Vol. 57, No. 1, 1995, pp. 289–300.

Berger, Mark, Dan Black, and Jeffrey Smith, "Evaluating Profiling as a Means of Allocating Government Services," in Michael Lechner and Friedhelm Pfeiffer, eds., *Econometric Evaluation of Active Labour Market Policies*, Heidelberg, Germany: Physica, 2001, pp. 59–84.

Bureau of Labor Statistics, "Employer Costs for Employee Compensation—March 2019," webpage, 2019a. As of August 5, 2019: https://www.bls.gov/news.release/pdf/ecec.pdf

Bureau of Labor Statistics, "Local Area Unemployment Statistics," webpage, 2019b. As of August 15, 2019: https://www.bls.gov/lau/stalt.htm

Cohen, Jacob, *Statistical Power Analysis for the Behavioral Sciences*, 2nd ed., Hillsdale, N.J.: Lawrence Erlbaum Associates, 1988.

Conway, Maureen, and Marshall Bear, *Asian Neighborhood Design: A Case Study of a Sectoral Employment Development Approach*, Washington, D.C.: Aspen Institute, June 1, 2000.

De Tray, Dennis N., *Veteran Status as a Screening Device*, Santa Monica, Calif.: RAND Corporation, P-6503, 1980. As of August 12, 2019: https://www.rand.org/pubs/papers/P6503.html

Duflo, Esther, William Gale, Jeffrey Liebman, Peter Orszag, and Emmanuel Saez, "Saving Incentives for Low- and Middle-Income Families: Evidence from a Field Experiment with H&R Block," *Quarterly Journal of Economics*, Vol. 121, No. 4, October 2005, pp. 1311–1346.

Eberts, Randall W., Christopher J. O'Leary, and Stephen A. Wandner, *Targeting Employment Services*, Kalamazoo, Mich.: W.E. Upjohn Institute for Employment Research, 2002.

Federal Reserve Bank of St. Louis, "Median Household Income in Louisiana," webpage, 2019. As of August 5, 2019: https://fred.stlouisfed.org/series/MEHOINUSLAA646N.

Glasmeier, Amy K., Candace Nelson, and Jeffery W. Thompson, *Jane Addams Resource Corporation: A Case Study of a Sectoral Employment Development Approach*, Washington, D.C.: Aspen Institute, December 2000.

Goos, Maarten, Alan Manning, and Anna Salomons, "Explaining Job Polarization: Routine-Biased Technological Change and Offshoring," *American Economic Review*, Vol. 104, No. 8, August 2014, pp. 2509–2526.

Heckman, James J.,"Policies to Foster Human Capital," *Research in Economics*, Vol. 54, No. 1, August 1999, pp. 3–56.

Heckman, James J., Carolyn J. Heinrich, and Jeffrey Smith, "Performance Standards and the Potential to Improve Government Performance," in James J. Heckman, Carolyn J. Heinrich, Pascal Courty, Gerald Marschke, and Jeffrey Smith, eds., *The Performance of Performance Standards*, Kalamazoo, Mich.: W. E. Upjohn Institute for Employment Research, 2011, pp. 1–14.

Heckman, James J., and Jeffrey A. Smith, "Assessing the Case for Social Experiments," *Journal of Economic Perspectives*, Vol. 9, No. 2, Spring 1995, pp. 85–110.

Heinrich, Carolyn, Peter R. Mueser, Kenneth R. Troske, Kyung-Seong Jeon, and Daver C. Kahvecioglu, "Do Public Employment and Training Programs Work?" *IZA Journal of Labor Economics*, Vol. 2, No. 1, 2013.

Hollenbeck, Kevin, *Study of Washington's Unemployment Training Benefits Program*, Kalamazoo, Mich.: W.E. Upjohn Institute for Employment Research, 2012.

Hollenbeck, Kevin, and Wei-Jang Huang, *Net Impact and Benefit-Cost Estimates of the Workforce Development System in Washington State*, Kalamazoo, Mich.: W. E. Upjohn Institute Technical Report No. 13-029, 2014.

Huber, Martin, *Statistical Verification of a Natural "Natural Experiment": Tests and Sensitivity Checks for the Sibling Sex Ratio Instrument*, St. Gallen, Switzerland: University of St. Gallen, School of Economics and Political Science Economics, Economics Working Paper Series 1219, 2012.

Imbens, Guido, and Joshua Angrist, "Identification and Estimation of Local Average Treatment Effects," *Econometrica*, Vol. 62, No. 2, March 1994, pp. 467–475.

Imbens, Guido, and Donald B. Rubin, "Estimating Outcome Distributions for Compliers in Instrumental Variables Models," *Review of Economic Studies*, Vol. 64, No. 4, October 1997, pp. 555–574.

Inserra, Anne, Maureen Conway, and John Rodat, *Cooperative Home Care Associates: A Case Study of a Sectoral Employment Development Approach*, Washington, D.C.: Aspen Institute, February 1, 2002.

Internal Revenue Service, "SOI Tax Stats-Historic Table 2," webpage, 2019. As of August 5, 2019:
https://www.irs.gov/statistics/soi-tax-stats-historic-table-2

Knowlton, Lisa W., and Cynthia C. Phillips, *The Logic Model Guidebook Better Strategies for Great Results*, 2nd ed., Thousand Oaks, Calif.: Sage Publications, 2012.

Kremer, Michael R., Edward Miguel, and Rebecca Thornton, "Incentives to Learn," *Review of Economics and Statistics*, Vol. 91, No. 3, August 2009, pp. 437–456.

LaLonde, Robert, "Evaluating the Econometric Evaluations of Training Programs with Experimental Data," *American Economic Review*, Vol. 76, No. 4, September 1986, pp. 604–620.

Levin, Henry M., and Patrick J. McEwan, *Cost-Effectiveness Analysis: Methods and Applications*, 2nd ed., Thousand Oaks, Calif.: Sage Publications, 2000.

Levitt, Steven D., and John A. List, "Viewpoint: On the Generalizability of Lab Behavior to the Field," *Canadian Journal of Economics*, Vol. 40, No. 2, May 2007a, pp. 347–370.

Levitt, Steven D., and John A. List, "What Do Laboratory Experiments Measuring Social Preferences Reveal About the Real World?" *Journal of Economic Perspectives*, Vol. 21, No. 2, Spring 2007b, pp. 153–174.

List, John A., and Imran Rasul, "Chapter 2: Field Experiments in Labor Economics," in Orley Ashenfelter and David Card, eds., *Handbook of Labor Economics*, Vol. 4, Part A, Amsterdam: North-Holland, 2011, pp. 103–228.

Louisiana Department of Children and Family Services, "Family Independence Temporary Assistance (FITAP)," webpage, undated a. As of August 5, 2019: http://www.dcfs.louisiana.gov/index.cfm?md=pagebuilder&tmp=home&nid=163 &pid=139

Louisiana Department of Children and Family Services, "Kinship Care Subsidy Program (KCSP)," webpage, undated b. As of August 5, 2019: http://www.dcfs.louisiana.gov/index.cfm?md=pagebuilder&tmp=home&nid=163 &pid=138

Louisiana Department of Children and Family Services, "Supplemental Nutrition Assistance Program (SNAP)," webpage, undated c. As of August 5, 2019: http://www.dcfs.louisiana.gov/index.cfm?md=pagebuilder&tmp=home&nid=326 &pid=93

Maguire, Sheila, Joshua Freely, Carol Clymer, Maureen Conway, and Deena Schwartz, *Tuning in to Local Labor Markets: Findings from the Sectoral Employment Impact Study*, Philadelphia, Pa., New York, N.Y., and Oakland, Calif.: Public/ Private Ventures, 2010.

Mardi Gras New Orleans, "Mardi Gras Indians," webpage, undated. As of August 13, 2019: https://www.mardigrasneworleans.com/history/mardi-gras-indians/

"National Green Infrastructure Certification Program," webpage, 2019. As of August 19, 2019: https://ngicp.org/

Patton, Michael Q., *Qualitative Research and Evaluation Methods*, 2nd ed., Thousand Oaks, Calif.: Sage Publications, 1990.

Pindus, Nancy M., Carolyn O'Brien, Maureen Conway, Conaway Haskins, and Ida Rademacher, *Evaluation of the Sectoral Employment Demonstration Program*, Washington, D.C.: Urban Institute, 2004.

Riemer, Manuel, and Leonard Bickman, "Using Program Theory to Link Social Psychology and Program Evaluation," in Melvin M. Mark, Stewart I. Donaldson, and Bernadette Campbell, eds., *Social Psychology and Evaluation*, New York: Guilford Press, 2011, pp. 104–140.

Rodner, Anne, Carol Clymer, and Laura Wyckoff, *Targeting Industries, Training Workers and Improving Opportunities*, Philadelphia, Pa., New York, N.Y., and Oakland, Calif.: Public/Private Ventures, 2008.

Roodman, David, James MacKinnon, Morten Nielsen, and Matthew Webb, "Fast and Wild: Bootstrap Inference in Stata Using Boottest," Kingston, Canada: Queen's Economics Department Working Paper No. 1406, 2018.

Rossi, Peter H., Mark W. Lipsey, and Howard E. Freeman, *Evaluation: A Systematic Approach*, 7th ed., Newberry Park, Calif.: Sage Publications, 2004.

Schochet, Peter Z., *Technical Methods Report: Guidelines for Multiple Testing in Impact Evaluations*, Washington, D.C.: U.S. Department of Education, Institute of Education Sciences, May 2008.

Schwartz, Heather L., and Lynn A. Karoly, *Cost Study of the Saint Paul Early Childhood Scholarship Program*, Santa Monica, Calif.: RAND Corporation, TR-947-SRI, 2011. As of August 13, 2019:
https://www.rand.org/pubs/technical_reports/TR947.html

"Social Aid and Pleasure Clubs," webpage, undated. As of May 5, 2015:
http://www.neworleansonline.com/neworleans/multicultural/multiculturaltraditions/socialaid.html

Tax Foundation, "Taxes in Louisiana," webpage, undated. As of August 5, 2019:
https://taxfoundation.org/state/louisiana

Thompson, Jeffery W., Susan Turner-Meikeljohn, and Maureen Conway, *Focus: HOPE: A Case Study of a Sectoral Employment Development Approach*, Washington, D.C.: Aspen Institute, 2000.

Van Horn, Carl, Tammy Edwards, and Todd Greene, eds., *Transforming U.S. Workforce Development Policies for the 21st Century*, Kalamazoo, Mich.: W. E. Upjohn Institute for Employment Research, 2015.

Wholey, Joseph S., Harry P. Hatry, and Kathryn E. Newcomer, *Handbook of Practical Program Evaluation*, 3rd ed., San Francisco, Calif.: Jossey-Bass, 2010.